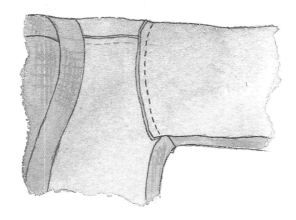

sewing classics

sewing classics

projects · techniques · motifs

Miriam Coe

Photography by Debbie Patterson

Quadrille

page 1: Jacket (see page 88)
page 2: Bags (see page 38)
page 3: Shirt (see page 65)
page 5: Duvet cover (see page 30)

Ilustrations • Lucy Su
Technical drawings • Stephen Dew
Detail photography • Dave King

First published in 1996 by
Quadrille Publishing Limited
9 Irving Street, London WC2H 7AT

Published in association with the National Magazine Company Limited
Country Living is a trademark of the National Magazine Company Limited

Copyright © Text, design and layout 1996 Quadrille Publishing Limited
Copyright © Project photography 1996 Debbie Patterson
Copyright © Detail photography 1996 Dave King

Art Director • Mary Evans
Project Editor • Hilary More
Copy Editor • Sarah Widdicombe
Editorial Assistant • Katherine Seely

British Library Cataloguing-in-Publication Data
A catalogue record for this book is available
from the British Library.

ISBN 1 899988 85 8

Printed in Spain

contents

Introduction

Not long ago, home sewing was an essential skill for all women, and most households possessed a sewing machine. While embroidery was a hobby, sewing was simply a job which had to be done.

Times have certainly changed. We now live our lives at an incredible pace, and the time that once was available for sewing has vanished. With the widespread availability of a huge variety of relatively cheap, mass-produced garments and home furnishings, the need has also disappeared – but there is another change in the air. Many people are coming back to sewing, but this time from choice and with the desire to make an individual statement in the way they dress and furnish their homes. Most importantly, they are finding renewed enjoyment in sewing, since instead of having to make everything, they can now select particular projects to stitch.

This book is designed to inspire those who already have a basic understanding of sewing and are looking for the skills to progress a little further. The first chapter looks at the equipment you will need and at the characteristics of particular fabrics. Some knowledge of these is essential to successful sewing, as it is heartbreaking to put in hours of work only to find that the finished item is a disaster simply because it has been made up in an inappropriate fabric.

Next comes seaming. This is the very foundation of sewing: the end result depends on good work at this stage, and it is important to choose the right seam for each job. A good range of flat seams is covered, plus three-dimensional construction and the use of gussets.

The following chapter looks at the important topic of fullness and how to control and dispose of it. Again, there are several ways of tackling each problem, with a choice of solutions available.

The final chapter deals with edges and finishings, and ways in which to embellish your work. This is the point at which you can let your imagination run free, using traditional trimmings in new and interesting ways to create a finished item that is truly your own.

Getting started

Successful sewing depends on choosing the right fabric, so before you pick up a needle it is essential to learn all about the different types and how to choose the right fabric for your project. Go and look at fabrics in the shops and handle them to gauge how they behave. Crush a corner of a fabric in your hand and let it unfold gently to see how it reacts; run it through your fingers and see how it feels. Before long you will be able to choose the right fabric for the job simply from its appearance and handling alone.

In this chapter we look at the origins of each fabric and how it is made, then describe its advantages and disadvantages and how to decide on a suitable one for a particular design. We also explain how to select exactly the right equipment to turn this fabric into a wonderful piece of stitching of which you can feel justly proud.

fabrics

The finished appearance, feel and behaviour of any fabric depends on the fibre or mix of fibres from which it is made, the way in which the fabric is constructed and any finishing processes which have been used. Fibres can be conviently divided into 2 main groups – those which are produced naturally and those which are man-made. The natural fibres can be sub-divided into another 2 groups – those from animal and those from vegetable sources. The man-made fibres can also be sub-divided into 2 main groups – those from natural sources and those from chemical sources.

Choosing fabrics

The range of fabrics available today is enormous and the task of making the right choice can be daunting. Before buying fabric, decide what weight and type would be suitable for the job in hand. Each roll of fabric should be labelled with its fibre content and care instructions, but if in doubt, ask for details before making your purchase.

Wool

Wool is a natural fabric made from yarn spun from the fleece or hair of a variety of animals including sheep, goats and camels. It is available in a wide range of weights, textures, weaves and qualities. Wool fabric can be smooth, plain, fleecy, textured, tweedy, crisp, thick, heavy, soft or delicate, depending on the effect desired. The description 'wool' used alone usually means that the fabric has been made from the fleece of a sheep – the other animal fibres are labelled with their names.

Worsted yarns, spun from the longer fibres, are smooth, tightly twisted and slightly stretchy and are woven into high-quality, hardwearing worsted fabric. Woollen yarns, spun from the shorter fibres, are softer, looser and slightly twisted, and are made into fabrics such as flannel.

Wool is a good-tempered and accommodating fabric which can be moulded into shape unlike any other. With careful use of pressing, garments can be made to follow the body's curved contours, and tailors make good use of these properties when creating well-fitting suits.

Woollen fabrics vary greatly, from the blanket-thick wool velours to delicate wool challis and nun's veiling. Not only is wool warm and comfortable to wear, it is also extremely beautiful. No other fabric can compare with the wonderful wool tweeds so beloved of today's fashion designers.

ADVANTAGES
• Wool is the warmest of all natural fabrics. The intrinsic crimp in the fibres traps air which, being a bad conductor of heat, helps to prevent body heat from escaping.
• Wool fibres are naturally flame resistant, the fibres smouldering rather than bursting into flame.
• The fibres' natural crimp allows them to resist wrinkling and return to their original shape after creasing.
• Wool fabric tailors well and is easy to shape using steam. Lightweight woollen fabrics are soft and will hang and drape well.
• The fibres hold colour well and can be dyed at any stage: fibre, yarn or fabric.

DISADVANTAGES
• Wool fibres are weaker when wet and, unless specially treated, may shrink. Care must be taken when washing, and the garment may need to be dry cleaned.
• Moths and carpet beetles attack wool, so precautions need to be taken when storing woollen fabrics.
• Light-coloured wool will become discoloured in strong light, eventually deteriorating with prolonged exposure.
• Wool can be expensive, so it is often blended with other fibres to reduce the cost and add strength and shrink resistance. Blending can also help to reduce the slightly itchy feel of some coarse wool fabrics, which may irritate sensitive skins.

Other animal fibres

Mohair Mohair comes from the coat of the Angora goat. The lightweight fibres are long and resilient and have an attractive sheen. Mohair fabric tends to be hairy in texture. It dyes very well – bright, jewel colours are often used. The fibres are also blended with wool to produce men's lightweight suiting fabrics.

Angora This soft, fluffy fibre comes from the fur of the Angora rabbit and is easily recognized by its distinctive sprinkling of white hairs.

Cashmere The fibre from the Cashmere goat produces a soft, luxurious fabric with a smooth, slippery feel. Pure cashmere is very expensive, and so is often blended. Cashmere is very warm yet light to wear.

Camel Camel-hair cloth is made from the soft inner coat of the camel. The fabric is warm, light, soft to the touch and very expensive, but the fibres may be blended with wool to reduce the cost. Camel hair fabric is nearly always camel coloured, ranging from creams to golden tans through to brown. The term 'camel cloth' is often used loosely to describe camel coloured coating which is usually made of wool and does not have the properties of real camel hair cloth.

Llama, alpaca and vicuna These closely related animals produce very soft, fine hair. Fibres from all of them are very expensive and much sought after as they make beautiful, luxurious fabrics. Again, they can be blended with wool or other fibres for economy.

Cotton

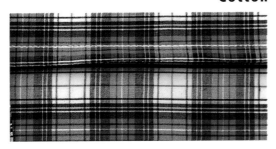

Cotton fabric has been produced from the downy seedpod fibres of the cotton plant for thousands of years and, even with the introduction of synthetics, is still the main textile used throughout the world. It is relatively cheap to produce and is a wonderfully easy-going fabric.

The fabric quality depends very much on fibre length, which in turn depends on both the plant variety and growing conditions. The longest fibres are the most expensive and produce the softest fabric. Sea Island and Egyptian cotton are some of the finest, while Indian cotton, with shorter fibres, produces a coarser but still attractive cloth.

Cotton fabric varies from the finest batiste to the heaviest drill. It is also successful as a knitted fabric, such as cotton jersey, which is used extensively for teeshirts, vests and jogging suits. Cotton is very easy to sew, so if you have never made anything before, this is the fabric with which to start.

ADVANTAGES
- Strong and hardwearing, cotton is easy to wash, and can be boiled and scrubbed to remove heavy soiling.
- Cotton fabric takes up and holds dyes well. It can also be woven or printed with colourful patterns.
- Soft, non-abrasive and absorbent, cotton is an ideal fabric for wearing next to the skin.
- Cotton fabric does not build up static cling, a major drawback of synthetics.

DISADVANTAGES
- Cotton creases in use, the creases remaining until they are ironed or washed out. However, this can largely be overcome by mixing with synthetics, for example in polycotton sheeting.
- Cotton fabrics are flammable and will flare when alight, so choose one which has been specially treated to be flame resistant when making night wear and children's garments.

Linen

Linen is one of the oldest fabrics, yet is still highly prized today for suits and shirts. It is made from the stem fibres of the flax plant, which grows well in cool, damp climates – the best linen comes from Ireland or Belgium.

Only a small range of fabrics is produced, most of the variations depending on the degree of coarseness: the finest are referred to as 'handkerchief' linens, while the heavier types are used for suits and jackets. Linen thread is also used for embroidery and is used to make lace. The fabric is easy to sew and presses beautifully – there is something extra special about neatly pressed, crisp white linen.

ADVANTAGES
- Linen is cool and absorbent, and is very comfortable to wear, especially in warm weather.
- It is extremely hardwearing and works well for outer garments, curtains and all types of furniture coverings.
- Linen fabrics have an attractive natural lustre and good shape retention, and are moth resistant.

DISADVANTAGES
- Linen creases easily, but can be treated with a crease-resistant finish to help avoid this problem.
- Pure linen is expensive, but can be mixed with cotton and synthetic fibres to reduce the cost and add a measure of crease resistance. Linen union, a popular choice for furnishings, is made from a blend of linen and cotton.

Other plant fibres
Ramie, also called China grass, is a soft, hairy fibre which looks rather like linen but is less expensive and easier to dye. It is usually blended with cotton or silk to make a lustrous fabric.

Jute, hemp, sisal, coir and kapok are also plant fibres. The first four are used to make floor coverings and rope, while kapok is used as a filling for soft toys.

Silk

Silk must be the queen of fabrics, and is probably the most luxurious and highly prized of all natural fibres. The silk is obtained from the caterpillar of the silk moth, which extrudes the threads from its head to wind around itself forming a cocoon. This fabric is unthreaded by man to make into silk fabric. Silk is one of the oldest fibres known to man and has been in continuous production for several thousand years.

Using different weaves, finishes and chemical treatments, silk can be made into a huge variety of different fabrics. It is difficult to believe that heavily textured silk tweed comes from the same source as the floaty, delicate chiffons, or that luxuriously smooth duchesse satin belongs to the same family as crisp, rustling taffeta.

Some silks can be expensive. The quality of the silk itself, together with the quality of the printing and exclusivity of the design, all contribute to the cost. However, there are silks to suit everyone's budget and good-quality silk is available at very reasonable prices.

The best silk is made from the long unbroken silk threads. If the threads break the short lengths are spun together to make spun silk.

Any waste silk from the cocoon is collected and spun into coarser yarns which are woven into heavier fabrics such as silk tweed. These fabrics do not have the drapability or sheen of more expensive silk. Wild silk, also known as tussore, tussah or shantung, is made from the silk produced by wild silkworms and has characteristic slubs running through the finished fabric.

Some silks may seem difficult to sew at first, but with a little bit of experience these difficulties are soon overcome and the end result makes all the effort more than worthwhile.

ADVANTAGES
- Silk fabrics are smooth, lustrous and attractive for both dressmaking and home furnishings.
- Although it can look delicate, silk is surprisingly strong.
- Silk is absorbent, which makes it comfortable to wear, and is also resistant to creasing.
- Silk dyes easily producing vivid colours.
- Silk is light in weight making it suitable for travelling.

DISADVANTAGES
- Some silk fabrics fray badly when they are cut, and sheer silks such as chiffon and georgette can also be quite difficult to sew.
- Silk requires great care when it comes to laundering.

Man-made fabrics

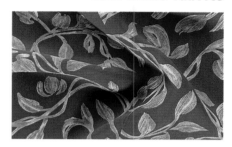

Man-made fabrics include those made from natural sources, such as wood pulp and waste cotton, which are unspinnable in their raw state. They are treated chemically and made into a liquid, which is then forced through holes and dried into a yarn, ready to make up into fabric.

Viscose Viscose was one of the first man-made fabrics to be produced in this country. Produced from wood pulp, viscose was formerly known as rayon. It has been improved greatly in recent years and now has good draping qualities. It is widely used for dresses and skirts, and is also mixed with other fibres, such as wool and cotton.

Acetate Acetate was the second fabric to appear on the market. It is made from waste cotton and/or wood pulp. It is not very strong. It is made into taffetas, satins and brocades. Linings are often made from acetate.

Synthetic fibres are made from substances which do not naturally form fibres but are synthesized. The main raw materials for these fibres are oil and petroleum products, and they are produced in much the same way as other man-made fibres.

Synthetic fabrics have come a long way since they were first introduced. Their great advantage is their ease of care. They are crease resistant, and can be crumpled up into a tiny space and emerge without a crease, making them ideal for holiday clothes and when travelling. Most are also easy to wash, quick to dry and do not need ironing, a real bonus with today's hectic lifestyles.

Nylon Nylon was the first truly synthetic fibre to be produced. It is very strong and fine. Nylon is used extensively in clothing fabrics, soft furnishings and upholstery.

Polyester One of the most versatile of the synthetic fibres, polyester is extremely strong and can be made into the finest of fabrics as well as some of the heaviest. It is often mixed with other fibres. Poly-cotton is perhaps the most well known mixture.

Acrylic Acrylic fibres are made from acrylonitrile. The fibres are soft and can be crimped to resemble wool. They are often used for blankets and knitwear, but acrylic fibres have many uses for dresses, suits, sportswear and fleecy linings.

ADVANTAGES
- Synthetic fabrics can be pleated permanently because of their plastic nature and the pleats will not fall out when washed.
- Most synthetic fabrics are crease resistant.
- They are also very strong and hardwearing.

DISADVANTAGES
- Synthetics are not quite as comfortable to wear as natural fibres.
- They can produce static cling.

equipment

Good equipment is absolutely essential in order to produce a professional-looking finish to your work. It also makes stitching much more of a pleasure. There are a few items which are essential in the workbasket, and a lot of gadgets that are helpful for home sewing and dressmaking. Buy the basics first, choosing the best you can afford. If treated with care, your sewing equipment will last for many years.

Pins

Pins can be made from steel, nickel plate, brass or stainless steel. Always choose the correct pins for the fabric you are using. Store pins in airtight boxes or in pincushions; a magnetic pin tray is useful for picking up dropped pins. Inspect pins before use and discard any blunt ones which might snag the fabric.

- **General dressmaking pins** For general use on medium- to heavyweight fabrics.
- **Fine pins** Perfect for fine fabrics, but tough fabrics will make them bend.
- **Extra-long, extra-fine pins** Very long pins for use on most fine fabrics.
- **Ballpoint pins** Round-ended pins for use with knitted fabrics.
- **Glass-headed pins** Expensive, but easy to see and pick up. A longer version is available, which is intended for use with heavier fabrics.
- **Lace pins** Usually made from brass and used when making and stitching lace.

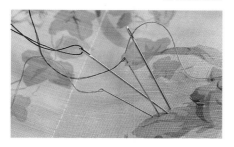

Needles

Several different types of hand-sewing needle are available, each designed for a particular task. Needles come in numbered sizes – the lower the number, the longer and fatter the needle. They must be sharp, so check before stitching and throw away any that are blunt or bent, or which show signs of rust.

You will need to keep a range of 'sharps' and 'betweens', plus a few 'straws', in your workbasket ready for hand sewing. The other needles mentioned below are required for specialist hand sewing and embroidery.

Sharps Medium-length needles with small, rounded eyes, used for general hand sewing.

Betweens (quilting needles) Short needles with small eyes, essential for fine hand sewing and tailoring.

Straws Very long, fine needles, useful for tacking and gathering.

Ballpoint needles Designed especially for use with knitted fabrics. The rounded end slides between the threads without snagging, which might cause puckering and ladders.

Darning needles Long needles, with large eyes that can cope with thick yarns. The length is necessary in order to span holes when darning.

Crewel needles Medium-length embroidery needles, with large, long eyes to allow several strands of embroidery cotton to be threaded together.

Bodkins Short, blunt needles which can be rounded or flat, with large eyes. They are used for threading elastic and ribbon through casings.

Thimbles

To help feed the needle through the fabric, you may like to use a thimble on the middle finger of your sewing hand. Choose a steel thimble in preference to one made from soft, easily pierced silver.

Threads

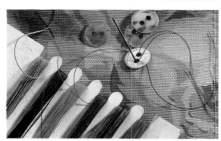

Choosing the correct thread will ensure a professional look and finish to your sewing projects. If possible, the thread should match the composition of the fabric in both fibre and weight, and be able to withstand the same washing and ironing temperatures, as the two elements cannot be treated differently once made up.

Choose a thread colour that matches the fabric. On a two-tone fabric, it is better to match the darker colour, because a single thread appears lighter when removed from the reel. Threads for both hand and machine sewing should be strong and of good quality, with a smooth finish. The higher the number on the spool, the finer the thread.

Beeswax is a useful addition to your workbasket. Pull the working thread through it to give extra strength and to prevent tangling when hand sewing.

Linen Very strong, and useful for sewing on buttons, but often too thick and too expensive for general sewing.

Silk Wonderfully smooth and shiny, but very expensive. It is ideal for stitching pure silk and is also good for sewing woollen garments, particularly when stitching by hand. Thicker silk threads are ideal for hand sewing buttonholes.

Cotton The most common of the natural threads. Much cheaper than silk or linen, it is usually 'mercerized' to make it smooth. Cotton and cotton-mix threads are suitable for sewing all natural fabrics.

Synthetic Usually made of polyester and available in a wide range of colours. Fine and strong, and suitable for most fabrics.

Tacking thread Soft, loosely twisted unmercerized cotton, available in black and white, which breaks very easily. This is important, as tacking threads need to be removed quickly and easily without tearing the fabric. Tacking thread is also quite hairy, which allows it to grip the fabric and stay in place until it is ready to be removed.

Invisible thread A nylon thread, virtually colourless to blend with any fabric.

Measuring equipment

You will need a dressmaker's tape measure and metre rule (yardstick).

Choose a plastic or fibreglass tape measure, but both will need renewing frequently, as they have a tendency to stretch and give inaccurate measurements.

A metre rule (yardstick) available in wood or plastic, is a useful and, in some circumstances, more accurate tool than a tape measure. Keep rulers clean, and wooden ones free of splinters.

Markers

A variety of fabric markers is available, ranging from special pens whose lines fade in the daylight or after several days, to various types of coloured crayon.

One of the best markers is traditional tailor's chalk, which comes in square and triangular shapes. Several colours are available, but white is the easiest to remove, using a brush. For fine, accurate lines, sharpen tailor's chalk using a scissors blade.

Scissors

Scissors must be sharp. They should be kept solely for cutting fabrics and threads, and should not be used for any other crafts which might blunt them. Try not to drop scissors on the floor, as this will damage the blades. Left-handed scissors are available in all the main types.

Dressmaking shears Essential for cutting out fabric. Invest in a good-quality pair of large, long-bladed shears and, with care, they will last for many years. The handles should be bent to one side, so that while cutting out the shears sit flat on the table. For more advanced work, it is a good idea to have two pairs – one for natural fibres and one for synthetics, as the latter quickly blunt the blades.
General sewing scissors Choose a medium-sized pair with straight handles, for trimming seams.
Small sewing scissors Short, very sharp points are essential for snipping threads, and for cutting into buttonholes and sharp corners.
Paper or craft scissors Keeping a pair of ordinary household scissors in your workbasket will remove the temptation to use your fabric scissors for cutting paper or card.
Rotary cutters Very sharp cutting wheels, particularly good for cutting straight pieces of fabric, such as bias strips or patchwork pieces, where accuracy is important. They must only be used with a special cutting mat.

Pressing equipment

Correct pressing is essential to achieve a really professional result, so good pressing equipment is vital. Make sure that your iron and ironing board are kept clean.

• A good heavyweight iron is essential. It can be a steam iron, but you can also make steam using damp pressing cloths.
• Muslin makes very good pressing cloths. Cut several, each approximately 1m (1yd) square. These can be doubled up to make the required thickness.
• A 'ham' is very useful for pressing anything with a curve, as it will ensure the curve does not flatten out and lose its shape. The ham has wool on one side for pressing woollen fabrics and cotton on the other for pressing cotton fabrics.
• Similar to a ham, a 'roll' is used for pressing seams. The iron will exert pressure on the stitches of the seam and not on the seam allowance, thus avoiding making an impression on the right side of the fabric.
• A velvet pressing board will prevent crushing the pile.
• A simple block of wood can be used to bang steam into a fabric. This technique is used to press in pleats and in tailoring. If a block is not available, use the back of a clothes brush.

sewing machines

Sewing machines have not only revolutionized home sewing but have also facilitated the mass production of ready-made clothes. They have become very sophisticated machines with a wide range of different models on the market, so choosing the right one can be a daunting task. A sewing machine is a costly investment, but choose wisely and it will last a lifetime.

Domestic overlocking machines have only been on the market for about 15 years. They save a lot of time as they can stitch, trim and neaten a seam in one action. An overlocker is not a substitute for a conventional sewing machine.

Sewing machines

With the wealth of electronic and computerized models available today, choosing a sewing machine can be difficult, and requires time and careful attention. Collect brochures and talk to other sewers; go to a reputable independent dealer, explain your sewing needs and ask for advice. Be sure to try out some of the machines yourself – a demonstrator can make every machine look easy to operate. Try threading the machine yourself, and change the bobbin and the needle. Take some of your own fabric with you, as a demonstrator will use easy materials.

Do not be taken in by all the gimmicks the sewing machine can perform: think realistically about your sewing needs and how many of these functions you will actually use in your stitching projects. Most people simply need a machine that will give them a good straight stitch, zigzag stitch and buttonhole.

Machine needles

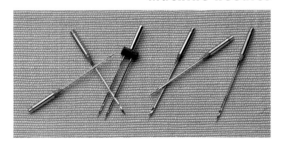

It is important to use the correct needle for each sewing project. It is also important to change needles frequently – machine needles become blunt surprisingly quickly, and as a result affect the smooth running of the machine. Various problems can then arise, including skipped stitches and snagged fabric. The timing of the machine can also be affected, so get into the habit of changing the needle before starting each new project.

Machine needles are available in numbered sizes. The lower the number, the finer the needle.

English/US	8	10	12	14	16
Continental	60	70	80	90	100

An 8 (60) needle is recommended for the finest fabrics, such as silk chiffon; a 16 (100) needle is suitable for the heaviest work.

A range of specialist needles for sewing machines is also available.

Overlockers can use sewing-machine needles or may require specialist needles, so check with the manufacturer.

Ballpoint needle Specially designed for knitted rather than woven fabrics, with a rounded end instead of a sharp point. The blunt end feeds between the threads instead of puncturing them, thereby minimizing the risk of laddering.

Jeans needle Very sharp point for penetrating closely woven fabrics, such as denim.

Leather needle Arrow-shaped point to pierce tough leather.

Twin needle Two needles on one shank, both of which are threaded. They make two absolutely parallel, equally spaced rows of stitching, perfect for pintucks and topstitching. Twin needles are available with different widths between the needles.

Triple needle Similar to a twin needle, but with three needles on one shank.

Wing needle Wider shank than standard needles, and used for decorative work.

Overlockers

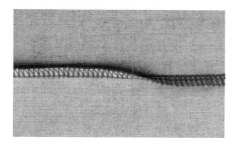

Overlocking machines are a relatively recent introduction. They do not take the place of conventional sewing machines, but are intended to be used in conjunction with them.

The primary function of an overlocker is to neaten raw edges with a professional finish, trimming off the fabric and then immediately overcasting the newly cut edges. Seams can thus be sewn, trimmed and overcast in one operation, saving hours of time. These seams are particularly useful on knitted fabrics, such as those used for sportswear, because they allow for a certain amount of stretch. They can also be used on woven fabrics with good results. In addition, some overlockers can be used for decorative stitching and to make rolled hems.

Overlocking machines are available with 2, 3, 4 or 5 threads. All overlockers cut and overcast edges at the same time, but the 4- and 5-thread machines make an extra row of stitching inside the overcast edge, creating a more secure seam. This is really only necessary on woven fabric, when it has not been seamed with a conventional machine. Most overlockers can be used with fewer threads than their maximum; for example, most 4-thread machines can make 2- or 3-thread overcast edges as well as the 4-thread seam.

Choosing an overlocker

As when choosing a conventional sewing machine, go to an independent and reputable dealer and explain your sewing needs. Take your own fabrics and try several models – overlockers are notoriously difficult to thread, so do try this out for yourself. You may need to make more than one visit.

Choosing threads

Overlockers use vast amounts of thread, which is available on huge cones. It is expensive to buy several cones of just the right colour to match all the different fabrics, so buy colours which blend rather than match, such as beiges and greys, plus black and white. Make sure the thread is strong. It will be put under a lot of strain in the overlocker, and if it breaks rethreading is very irksome. The thread must also be fine, as the volume of stitching could otherwise make the seams too bulky. Decorative threads are also available.

Plain & fancy seams

Seams are the basis of everything you make and it is important that you choose the right seam and make it as skilfully as possible, as the finished effect depends on it. Saris and sarongs may not need seams as they are simply lengths of fabric draped around the body. Similarly, throws used to cover chairs may not have seams; however these are the exceptions.

Seams are used to join narrow widths of fabrics, for curtains or bedlinen. The duvet cover has been made in this way and has straight seams which are cleverly disguised and emphasised with broderie Anglaise.

Seams can also give shape or form to a garment. The kimono shows seams being used to join simple, angular shapes to create a loose fitting garment, while the skirt seams have been shaped to fit the body. Seams are also used to make three-dimensional shapes, and these can incorporate a gusset. The bags and bench cushion use this technique.

plain seams

Fabrics are seamed or joined together to make a wider piece of fabric or to give shape. Most seams are therefore functional. When choosing which seam to use, the type of fabric, the article or garment being made, the amount of wear and washing, together with the general finished effect, should all be taken into consideration. Different seams can be used in the same project, depending on their position.

Plain, flat seam

This is the most commonly used seam. It is easy to make and gives a good flat finish, but with only one row of stitching it is not very strong. After stitching, the seam allowances are pressed open to either side of the seam.

1 With right sides together and cut edges matching, pin the two pieces of fabric together, placing the pins at right angles to the edge. Tack the two fabrics together along the seamline.

2 Machine stitch the fabrics together along the seamline. Press the machine stitching and then press the seam open. Trim and neaten the seam if necessary, following one of the methods below.

Neatening edges

As the cut edges of a plain, flat seam are exposed on the wrong side, they might require neatening to prevent them from fraying and to give a neater appearance. There are various ways of doing this, either by machine or by hand. Check that the method of neatening is appropriate to the fabric and project.

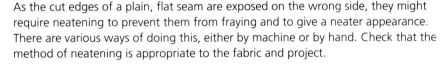

Zigzag This simple method of neatening is worked on the sewing machine, with a zigzag stitch made over the cut edge. The zigzag width and length can be altered for different effects. This method is especially useful for thick, firm or knitted fabrics.

Overlocking This method of neatening is worked on an overlocking machine (see page 21), either before or after stitching the seam using an ordinary sewing machine. It is very effective in preventing fraying, particularly on fabrics such as silk dupion, and can give quite a professional finish. As the overlocking threads are very fine, the result is a neat finish.

Machine stitching On firm, lightweight fabrics, such as cottons, the cut edges can be machine finished. Turn under the cut edge of each allowance for 3mm (⅛in) and press, then stitch close to the folded edge. As there are two layers of fabric, this method is not suitable for thick fabrics.

Hand stitching This is often preferable to machine stitching as a method of neatening. Careful hand stitching will blend in with the fabric and will not distort the seam. Two stitches are generally used:
Overcasting – work from left to right, making slanting stitches over and over the cut edge (fig 1). Do not pull the stitching too tight.
Blanket stitch – work from left to right. Insert the needle through the fabric and bring it out under the edge and over the working thread. Pull the thread through, forming a stitch on the edge of the seam allowance (fig 2). Again, do not pull the stitching too tight.

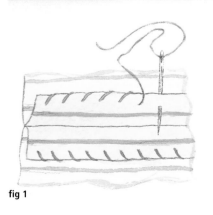

fig 1

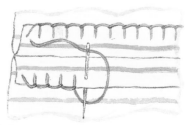

fig 2

French seam

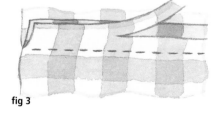

A French seam is self neatening, as the cut edges are enclosed within. Two rows of machine stitching make this seam stronger than a plain, flat seam.

French seams are only suitable for medium- and lightweight or sheer fabrics, as the extra thickness would be too great on heavier ones. French seams work best on straight seams and are particularly useful on fine fabrics, where the seam can show through to the right side, for example on chiffon.

1 With wrong sides together and cut edges matching, pin and tack the two pieces of fabric together.
2 Stitch the seam with a 1cm (⅜in) seam allowance. Remove the tacking threads.
3 Press the stitching. Press the seam allowance to one side and then trim down both of the seam allowances to 3mm (⅛in).

4 Refold the seam with the right sides of the fabric together and, using finger and thumb, manipulate the fabric so that the machine stitching is right on the edge. Pin, tack and stitch 6mm (¼in) from the folded edge.
5 Remove the tacking stitches. Press the machine stitching and then press the seam to one side.

Machine-felled seam

This is a very useful self-neatening seam. It uses two rows of machine stitching, so is strong. A machine-felled seam lies flat and looks as neat on the wrong side of the fabric as on the right.

1 With right sides together and cut edges matching, pin, tack and stitch the two pieces of fabric together as for a plain, flat seam. Remove the tacking and press the seam.
2 Trim down one of the seam allowances to 6mm (¼in) (fig 3). Press both seam allowances to one side, with the trimmed one underneath. Ensure you are consistent throughout, pressing the seams to either the front or the back.
3 Fold the cut edge of the wider seam allowance over and under the narrow one (fig 4), and tack this folded edge down on to the main fabric.
4 Stitch close to the folded edge, keeping parallel with the first row of stitches (fig 5). Remove the tacking.

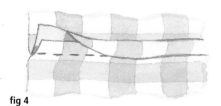

fig 3

fig 4

fig 5

Double-machined seam

This seam is a machine-felled seam worked on the right side of the fabric, so that both rows of stitching are visible. The stitching can be worked in a contrasting colour for added decoration.

It is very important that the two rows of stitching look exactly the same, so use the same stitch size throughout. As the upper and lower stitches on the machine are not exactly the same, care must be taken to ensure that it is the lower thread which is folded out of sight and the upper thread which is visible on the right side.

To make the seam, follow the instructions for the machine-felled seam, but begin by placing the wrong sides of the fabric together.

decorative seams

Seams are functional, but they can also be decorative and, with a bit of imagination, can be made a feature of the project. Making a seam more conspicuous often involves using another row of stitching, and this immediately makes the seam stronger. Note that when working a line of machine stitching on the right side of a garment or furnishing project, care must be taken to be very accurate, keeping the same distance from the seamline to the stitching throughout. Before stitching, check the stitch size on a similar fabric.

Welt seam

This is a variation on the machine-felled seam and is used on heavier fabrics where a machine-felled seam would be too bulky. The extra row of stitching is visible from the right side and adds both strength and decoration.

1 With right sides together and cut edges matching, pin, tack and stitch the two pieces of fabric together as for a plain, flat seam. Remove the tacking and press the seam to one side.
2 Trim down the inner seam allowance to 6mm (¼in). Neaten the wider seam allowance if necessary (fig 1).
3 Working from the right side, tack through the fabric and the wider seam allowance, enclosing the trimmed edge. Again working from the right side, topstitch down beside the seam (fig 2), catching in the wider seam allowance.

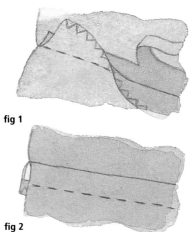

fig 1

fig 2

Tucked and overlaid seams

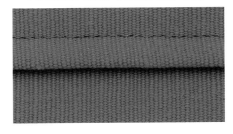

Tucked and overlaid seams are made in the same way. Neat and decorative, their final row of stitching is on the right side. Machine stitch close to the fold for an overlaid seam or 6mm (¼in) away for a tucked seam.

1 Mark seamlines on both fabrics.
2 Turn the seam allowance of the top fabric to the wrong side. Press and tack.
3 Place the top fabric on the bottom fabric, matching the folded edge to the marked seamline. Pin and tack in position. Stitch, parallel to and 3–6mm (⅛–¼in) from the fold (fig 3).

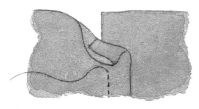

fig 3

Topstitched seam

This is a variation on a plain, flat seam, with two rows of stitching added on either side of the seamline for decoration.

1 With right sides together and cut edges matching, pin, tack and stitch the two pieces of fabric together as for a plain, flat seam. Press the seam open.
2 Working from the right side, topstitch the required distance from the seam along one side.
3 Working in the same direction, repeat step 2 on the other side, making sure the distance from the seam to the topstitching is the same. Use the presser foot as a guide to position the stitching.

Piped seam

There are two kinds of piped seam – soft and corded. Piping consists of a strip of fabric folded lengthways, which is sewn into a seam so that the fold of the piping is visible for decoration. If it is to be inserted into a curved or shaped seam it will need to be cut on the cross. Cord of various thicknesses can be sewn into the piping before it is stitched into a seam for a more defined look.

Soft piped seam

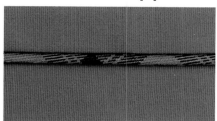

1 Fold the fabric strip in half lengthways with wrong sides together. Place the folded piping on the right side of one of the pieces of the fabric. Pin and tack along the seamline (fig 4).

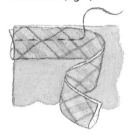

fig 4

2 Place the second piece of fabric over the first, with right sides together matching the cut edges. Pin, tack and machine stitch along the seamline (fig 5). Remove the tacking and press.

fig 5

Corded piped seam

A corded piped seam is made in the same way as a soft piped seam, but a length of cord is inserted inside the fold of the fabric strip. This is tacked and stitched in place before the corded piping is attached to the main fabric (fig 6). A zip foot or special piping foot on the machine will enable you to stitch close to the cord.

fig 6

Insertion seam

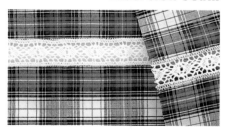

For this decorative seam, the fabrics to be joined are positioned at a distance from each other and bridged by a specially designed insertion, which is usually made of lace or broderie Anglaise. If the insertion has a specially finished edge, it is usually positioned on top of the fabric so that the edge can be seen. If it does not have a good edge, it is placed behind the fabric. Insertion seams can be straight or zigzag stitched. A mock insertion can be made by covering a seam with broderie Anglaise.

Straight-stitch insertion

1 Make a narrow hem on the edge of both pieces of fabric.
2 Lay the insertion on top of the right side of the pieces of fabric. Pin, tack and stitch in place.

Zigzag-stitch insertion

1 Lay the insertion right side up on the right side of one piece of fabric, so that the edge covers the fabric by 6mm (¼in). Pin and tack.
2 Stitch with a small, closely worked zigzag (fig 7) following any pattern on the edge of the insertion. Trim back the fabric to the zigzag stitches.
3 Lay the other edge of the insertion over the other side of the fabric in the same way. Pin, tack and zigzag in place (fig 8). Trim away the excess fabric.

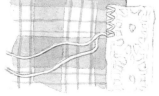

fig 7

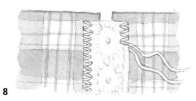

fig 8

bedlinen

A fine, soft cotton lawn makes the most luxurious bedlinen. Although the fabric may need to be joined to make it wide enough for a duvet cover, you can make a feature of the joins by adding broderie Anglaise insertion to cover the seams.

Square pillow case with lace insertion

Square pillows are becoming increasingly popular, but there is still only a small choice of ready-made pillowcases available, so making your own is a viable option. The central square is held on to the mitred edge with insertion lace and the whole case is edged with a deep mitred border.

fig 1

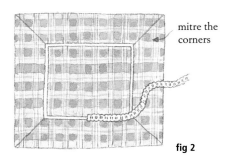

mitre the corners

fig 2

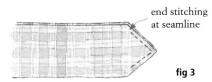

end stitching at seamline

fig 3

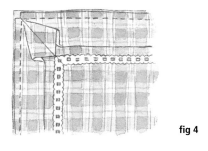

fig 4

fig 5

You will need
1.4m (1½yd) cotton, 90cm (36in) wide
1.6m (1¾yd) broderie Anglaise eyelet
   lace, 2cm (¾in) wide, for insertion
Matching sewing thread
1.6m (1¾yd) gingham ribbon, 6mm
   (¼in) wide

To cut out
1 For the front, cut out from cotton fabric 1 piece 37cm (14½in) square, and 4 pieces each 50 x 8cm (19¾ x 3⅛in) for the mitred inner border.
2 For the back, cut out from cotton fabric 1 piece 51 x 50cm (20⅛ x 19¾in), 1 piece 50 x 17cm (19¾ x 6¾in) for the flap, and 4 strips each 60 x 12cm (23¾ x 4¾in) for the outer border.

To make the front
1 Lay out the first inner border strip with the right side uppermost. Fold up one end diagonally so that the cut edges match, and press. Unfold and cut along the pressed line (fig 1). Repeat to mitre the opposite end of the strip in the same way, but folding so that the cut edge points in the opposite direction. Mitre all the border pieces in the same way.
2 With right sides together, join the inner border strips to form a square, taking a 1cm (⅜in) seam allowance. Press the seams open. Turn under the inner edge all round for 1cm (⅜in) and topstitch.
3 Press under the outer edge all round the front central square piece for 1cm (⅜in) and topstitch.
4 Lay the central square right side up. Place the inner border right side up around the square, with corners matching. Mitring each corner, pin the

broderie Anglaise lace around the square and the border (fig 2), just overlapping the edges of both. Join the ends of the lace together. Tack and topstitch the lace in place along both edges.
5 Thread the ribbon around the insertion and knot the ends together at a corner.

To make and join on the outer border
1 Press the first outer border strip in half lengthways with wrong sides facing. At each end, fold up the cut edges diagonally to match the folded edge and press. Unfold and cut along the pressed line. Repeat with each border strip.
2 With the strips unfolded and right sides together, join them together to form a square, taking a 1cm (⅜in) seam allowance (fig 3). Turn to the right side and refold in half. Press.
3 Pin and tack the cut edges of the outer border to the pillowcase front with right sides together (fig 4).

To make up
1 Stitch a 6mm (¼in) double hem along one edge of the flap, and a 1cm (⅜in) double hem along one short edge of the back section.
2 Pin the back over the front with right sides together, the back hem edge adjoining the seamline at one side and the remaining cut edges matching.
3 Position the flap over the hemmed edge of the back pillowcase, matching the cut edge to the cut edge of the front and the side edges to the cut edges of the front and back. Pin, tack and stitch all round (fig 5).
4 Turn the pillowcase right side out, tucking the flap inside and press.

duvet cover The seams on a duvet cover need to be strong to withstand wear and tear and repeated washing. Adding a row of mock insertion over each seam means that the seams are made strong and secure by the two rows of topstitching that are added.

fig 1

fig 2

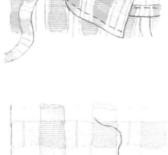

fig 3

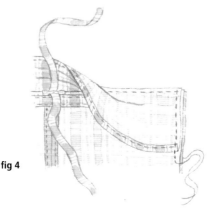

You will need

9.7m (10¾yd) main fabric, 90cm (36in) wide

Matching sewing thread

4.5m (4¾yd) broderie Anglaise insertion, 6cm (2½in) wide

4.5m (4¾yd) ribbon, 6mm (¼in) wide and safety pin (optional)

To cut out

1 For the front, cut out 1 piece 237cm (95¼in) x the fabric width, and 2 side front pieces each 237 x 27cm (100 x 10½in).

2 For the back, cut out 1 piece 206.5cm (81⅝in) x the fabric width, and 2 side back pieces each 206.5 x 27cm (81⅝ x 10½in).

3 Cut out 10 ties, each 26 x 2.5cm (10¼ x 1in).

To make the front

1 Join the side front pieces to the centre front piece with a plain, flat seam and neaten. Cut off a piece of fabric 34cm (14in) deep from the bottom of the front piece for the flap.

2 Place the broderie Anglaise centrally over the seams on the front, right side up. Pin, tack and stitch in place (fig 1).

3 If adding ribbon, cut into 2 equal lengths. Fasten one end of the first length on to a safety pin and thread the ribbon through the broderie Anglaise. Repeat for the second length.

4 Make the ties by folding the tie strips in half lengthways with right sides together and machine stitching 6mm (¼in) from the long cut edges. Turn the ties right side out and press. Tuck in 6mm (¼in) at one end of each tie and slip stitch to close. Make up 5 pairs of ties in this way.

5 With right sides together and the cut ends of the ties matching the cut edge of the front, position 5 ties equally

spaced along the bottom edge of the front.

6 Make a 2.5cm (1in) hem along one long edge of the flap piece and stitch in place. Position the flap on the front piece along the bottom edge, with right sides together. Pin, tack and stitch the flap in place, sandwiching the ties between the front and the flap (fig 2).

To make the back

1 Join the side back pieces to the centre back piece in the same way as for the front piece. Press up a 2.5cm (1in) double hem along the bottom edge.

2 Unfold the hem and, with right sides together and the cut ends of the remaining 5 ties placed to the cut edge of the back, position the ties on the back piece so that they correspond with the front. Pin and tack the ties, then refold the hem with the ties incorporated (fig 3). Stitch the hem along the fold and along the edge.

To make up

1 With right sides facing, place the front and back pieces of the cover together, keeping the flap out of the way and butting the hem of the back up to the flap seam.

2 Replace the flap over the back, then pin, tack and stitch the sides and top edge of the cover (fig 4), stitching through the flap sides. Press, and turn the cover right side out. Insert your duvet into the cover; tuck in the flap and fasten the ties.

fig 4

kimono

The kimono originated in Japan. There it is worn for both day and evening, sometimes made up in the most sumptuous fabrics. We have adopted its simple shape and combined stripes and checks in fashionable red and white, to create the perfect garment for lazy days spent relaxing at home.

You will need

4m (4¼yd) main fabric, 115cm (45in) wide
70cm (28in) contrast fabric, 90cm (36in) wide
Matching sewing threads
Paper for patterns

To scale up the patterns

Draw up the patterns for the kimono using the measurements shown on the shapes below.

To cut out

From main fabric
1 back
2 fronts
2 sleeves
From contrast fabric
2 cuffs
2 collars
2 sash pieces

To make the hanger and join front and back

1 Cut out a strip of contrast fabric 10 x 3cm (4 x 1¼in) and fold it in half lengthways with right sides together. Stitch 6mm (¼in) from the long cut edge. Turn right side out and press.

2 Fold the strip into an arrow shape and position at the centre of the neck on the wrong side of the back piece, with both cut edges against the cut edge of the neck. Tack the hanger in place (fig 1).

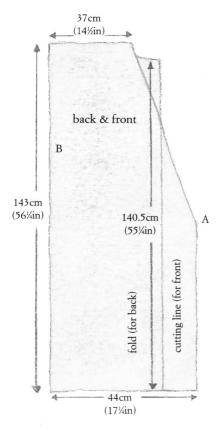

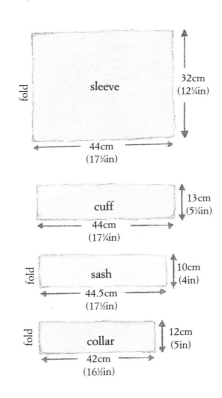

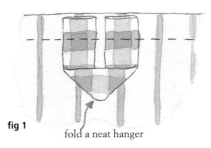

fig 1   fold a neat hanger

3 Join the front and back pieces at the shoulders with French seams.

4 Make a small double 6mm (¼in) hem down the centre fronts from point A to the hem edge and stitch in place.

To make and attach the collar

1 Join the 2 collar pieces at centre back and press. Press the seam allowance on both short edges of the collar to the wrong side.

2 Fold the collar in half lengthways with wrong sides together and press. Open the fold and press the seam allowance along one of the long edges to the wrong side.

3 With right sides together, join the unpressed long edge of the collar to the main body, matching points A in the front and seam to the centre back. Press the seam towards the collar and grade if necessary.

4 Refold the collar in half along the pressed fold, taking the collar over to the wrong side of the main body.

5 Butt the folded seam allowance against the first line of machine stitching. Pin and tack in position, then slip stitch in place, catching the stitches into the machine stitching.

6 Slip stitch the ends of the collar.

To join on the sleeves

1 With right sides together, pin, tack and stitch one long edge of each cuff to the lower edge of each sleeve. Press the seams towards the cuffs.

2 Join each sleeve to the main body with a French seam, matching the centre point at the top of the sleeve with the shoulder seam and stopping 1.5cm (⅝in) from either end of the sleeve (fig 2).

Press the seams towards the sleeves.

3 Join the side seams of the body, stopping at point B.

4 Join the sleeves, starting at point B and stitching up the ends of the sleeves.

5 Turn under the remaining raw edge of the cuffs and slip stitch in place, catching the stitches into the machine stitching in the same way as for the collar (fig 3).

To make the sash

1 Join the sash pieces. Trim and press.

2 Fold the sash in half lengthways with right sides together and stitch the long edges together.

3 Turn the sash right side out and press with the seam over the centre. Turn in the ends and slip stitch. Press.

To make the carriers

1 Cut a strip of contrasting fabric 20 x 4cm (8 x 1½in). Fold it in half lengthways with right sides together and stitch 6mm (¼in) from the long cut edge. Turn the strip right side out and press with the seam over the centre.

2 Cut the strip into 10cm (4in) lengths. Fold under both ends of each carrier.

3 Pin the carriers in position on the main body and stitch in place with a square of stitching at each end (fig 4).

To finish

Turn up a 2.5cm (1in) hem on the lower edge; tuck under the cut edge for 6mm (¼in) and stitch in place.

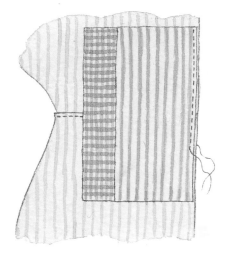

fig 2

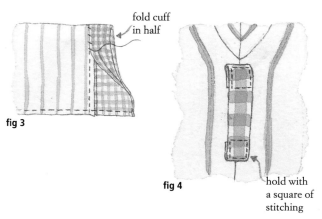

fold cuff in half

fig 3

fig 4

hold with a square of stitching

curves &
box shapes

Shaping and depth is achieved with curved seams and gussets. Curved seams need to be stitched with care, so that the seam allowance remains constant and the stitching flows smoothly around the shape. Once stitched, the seam allowance must be clipped and notched so that the seam can be pressed flat.

A gusset is the strip of fabric that provides depth between two shaped pieces. It can be as narrow as 2cm (¾in), or wide – say 10cm (4in) on a deep cushion. Gussets can be cut on the straight or on the bias of the fabric, depending on the gusset depth and the effect required. Cut gusset strips in one long length, or in sections to accommodate openings.

Curved seams

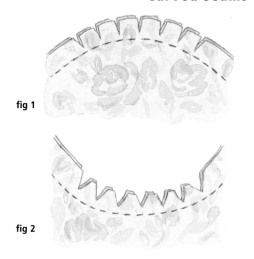

fig 1

fig 2

To make a curved seam, the two fabrics are placed together in the usual way for plain flat seams, using the appropriate seam allowance for the item. Set the sewing machine to a normal straight stitch and work slowly to achieve the necessary smooth and accurate stitching.

1 Place the two fabrics together with right sides facing and pin at regular intervals, with the pins positioned at right angles to the edge. Tack, then stitch with the appropriate seam allowance, feeding the fabric gently through the machine and guiding it around the curved edge.
2 To finish outward curves, where the seam allowance needs to spread out in order to lie flat, snip into the allowance up to the seamline (fig 1). Ensure that the snips are regularly spaced, and fit in

as many as necessary to allow the seam to be pressed flat. Neaten the cut edges with a zigzag stitch on the sewing machine.
3 To finish inward curves, snip out evenly spaced notches from the seam allowance, so that when the fabric is pressed it can overlap and lie flat (fig 2). To avoid weakening the seam unnecessarily, stagger the notches on either side of the seamline. Neaten the cut edges with a zigzag stitch on the sewing machine.

Circular box shapes

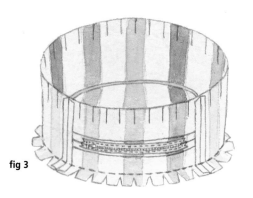

fig 3

Circular box shapes consist of top and bottom sections plus a gusset strip to cover the side edge. On large, circular pieces such as a deep cushion, a zip can be fitted into a section of the gusset strip before it is inserted between the top and bottom sections.

1 Cut one gusset strip to the circumference of the circle plus twice the seam allowance. With right sides together, join the strip into a ring. Snip into the seam allowance along both edges. With right sides facing, pin, tack and stitch the gusset to the top and bottom pieces, leaving an opening in one seam for turning. Insert the pad and close the opening.
2 To add a zip, measure the length of the zip and cut a gusset strip to size

adding twice the seam allowance, plus four times the seam allowance wider than the required depth.
3 Place the zip gusset pieces right sides together, and pin and tack down the whole length. Stitch from each end, leaving a central opening for the zip. Press the seam open. Lay the zip over the wrong side of the seam behind the tacked section. Pin, tack and stitch down both sides of the zip. Partially open the zip, then stitch the gusset in place (fig 3).

Box shapes · Box shapes are dealt with in the same way as circular box shapes, with the addition of a gusset strip. On a deep cushion, a zip is stitched between two folded gusset strips before it is inserted between the top and bottom sections. Deep gussets are usually cut on the straight grain and can run all round the shape with just one join, or be fitted together with seams to give sharp, crisp corners.

1 Measure the edges of the shape and cut one gusset strip to the length of each side plus twice the seam allowance x the depth of the shape plus twice the seam allowance.

2 Join the gusset strips together into a square or rectangle, beginning and ending the seams 1.5cm (⅝in) from each edge of each strip.

3 With right sides together, pin, tack and stitch the top section to the top edge of the gusset strip. Spread open the strip at each corner and then stitch, forming sharp corners.

4 Repeat, to stitch the bottom edge of the gusset strip to the bottom section, leaving a large opening centrally in one side. Trim, and then turn the cover right side out.

5 Insert the pad, turn in the opening edges and slip stitch together to close.

6 To set in a zip, measure the length of the zip and cut two strips to this length plus twice the seam allowance x the depth of the shape plus twice the seam allowance. Fold each strip in half lengthways with wrong sides together and press. Place the zip in the centre of these two pieces and tack and stitch it in position. Then make up the shape in the same way as before (fig 4), but without leaving an opening. Open the zip partially before stitching in the gusset strip (fig 5).

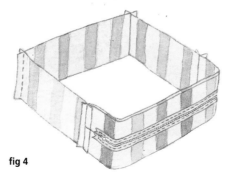

fig 4

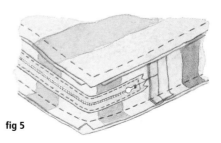

fig 5

Piped box shapes Plain or corded piping is often added on either side of the gusset strip to provide emphasis or a touch of colour or pattern to a plain shape. Cut the piping strip on the bias of the fabric.

1 Measure the length of the gusset strip and make up two lengths of piping to this length plus 4cm (1½in) for joining. Pin, tack and stitch each length of piping around the top and bottom sections.

2 Snip into the piping fabric at each corner on both square and rectangular shapes, On circular shapes, snip into the piping fabric all round at regular intervals so that the piping curves smoothly round the shape.

3 Join the ends of the piping together neatly to fit, positioning the join in the centre of the back on square and rectangular shapes.

4 Join the gusset to the top and bottom sections and if required, a zip can be added as before.

bags

Bags are an essential part of any wardrobe, whether for travelling or just shopping. A roomy saddle bag with wide, comfortable shoulder straps and a neat topstitched front pocket will hold all the bits and pieces essential for everyday life, while the carpet bag is perfect for around town or weekend jaunts in the country. Choose a hardwearing fabric that not only looks good but is substantial enough for a bag that needs to hold its shape under pressure. To add strength and a fashionable finish, quilt the fabric before making it up into a bag.

Saddle bag

Stamp your own style on a flower-strewn shoulder bag with curved seams and a topstitched pocket.

You will need
1m (1¼yd) main fabric, 115cm (45in) wide
1m (1¼yd) lining, 115cm (45in) wide
1m (1¼yd) interlining, 90cm (36in) wide
Matching sewing threads

To scale up the patterns
Draw up the patterns for the saddle bag using the measurements shown on the shapes on page 40.

To cut out
From main fabric
1 back
1 front
1 pocket
2 handles
1 gusset
From lining
Cut out the same pieces as for the main fabric, omitting the handles.
From interlining
Cut out the same pieces as for the main fabric, but cutting only one handle.

To prepare the fabric
Place an interlining piece on the wrong side of each fabric piece, interlining one handle piece only. Tack, keeping the fabric and interlining pieces flat.

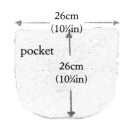

26cm
(10¼in)

pocket

26cm
(10¼in)

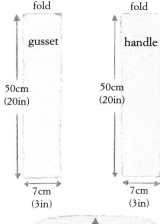

fold   fold

gusset   handle

50cm   50cm
(20in)   (20in)

7cm   7cm
(3in)   (3in)

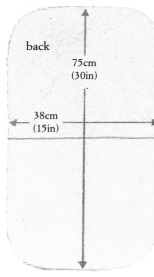

back

75cm
(30in)

38cm
(15in)

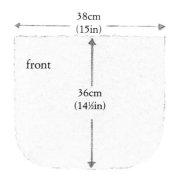

38cm
(15in)

front

36cm
(14½in)

To make and attach the pocket

1 With right sides together, pin and tack the pocket lining to the interlined pocket piece. Stitch, leaving a small gap to turn through.

2 Trim the seam and turn right side out. Slip stitch the gap closed and press. Topstitch across the top of the pocket close to the edge.

3 Position the pocket on the right side of the bag front, 7cm (3in) in from the sides and 7cm (3in) up from the bottom edge (fig 1). Pin, tack and topstitch the pocket in place.

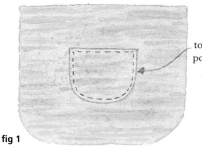

topstitch
pocket in
place

fig 1

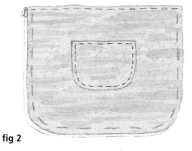

fig 2

To make the front

1 With right sides together, join the front lining to the interlined front piece along the top edge. Press; trim the seam and turn to the right side.

2 Topstitch along the top edge, then tack the rest of the front lining to the front piece, with wrong sides together and matching the cut edges (fig 2).

To make the back

1 With right sides together, place the back lining on the interlined back piece. Pin, tack and stitch together only around the flap.

2 Trim and clip the seam, clipping into the stitching at the end. Turn to the right side and press, then topstitch around the flap close to the edge.

3 Lay the rest of the lining over the rest of the back piece with wrong sides together and tack.

To make the handle

1 Turn under and press 1.5cm (⅝in) at the short ends of the interlined handle piece.

2 With right sides together, join the 2 handle pieces along the long edges.

3 Trim the seams; turn right side out and press. Topstitch along both long edges.

To join on the gusset and complete

1 With right sides facing, join the short ends of the handle to the gusset piece, being careful not to catch the turned-under ends in the stitching.

2 With right sides together, join the gusset to the front and back pieces of the bag. The front and back linings should be included in the seams.

3 Turn under 1.5cm (⅝in) at both short ends and along one long edge of the gusset lining and press.

4 Join the unfolded long edge of the gusset lining to the front of the bag, so that the gusset lining and the right side of the front lining are facing. The front of the bag will now be sandwiched between the gusset and the gusset lining. Clip, trim and press the seams towards the gusset.

5 Bring the gusset lining over the gusset and slip stitch the folded long edge of the gusset lining to the machine stitching of the other gusset seam.

6 Stitch the folded short ends of the handle to the short ends of the gusset lining. Turn the bag right side out.

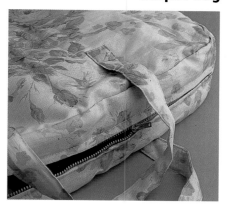

Carpet bag

This classic carpet bag can be made up in a strong pile fabric, backed with lining to give it added style and stability, or from a strong quilted cotton. Generous-size handles make the bag easy to carry.

You will need

1.2m (1⅜yd) main fabric, 137cm (54in) wide
1.2m (1⅜yd) lining fabric, 137cm (54in) wide
Matching sewing threads
75cm (30in) zip

To scale up the patterns

Draw up the patterns for the carpet bag using the measurements shown on the shapes on page 43.

To cut out

From main fabric
2 bags
2 handles
2 zip gussets
2 gussets
From lining
Cut out the same pieces as for the main fabric, omitting handles and zip gussets

To make the handles

1 With right sides together, fold both handle pieces in half lengthways, matching the cut edges together. Pin, tack and stitch along the long edges.
2 Trim the seam, turn both handles to the right side and press. Turn in the ends and slip stitch. Press.

To make the front and back

1 With wrong sides together, tack the front and back linings to the main pieces.
2 Position the handles 11cm (4½in) down from top edge and 17cm (6¾in) in from side edges. Stitch in a square at each end to secure (fig 1).

To insert the zip

1 With wrong sides together, fold both zip gusset pieces in half lengthways.
2 Fold under 1.5cm (⅝in) along one of the long edges of each piece.
3 Position the folded edges of the zip gusset pieces so that they meet together over the zip (fig 2); pin, tack and stitch.

To make and join on the gusset

1 With right sides together, join the gusset pieces along one short end and press the seam open.
2 With right sides together, join this plain gusset piece to the zip gusset along the short ends. Press the seams towards the gusset without the zip.
3 With right sides together, join the gusset to the front and back bag pieces, keeping the folded edges of the zip gusset out of the way.
4 Clip the seams up to the stitching where the zip and plain gussets meet.

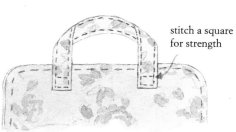

stitch a square
for strength

fig 1

fold gusset
in half

fig 2

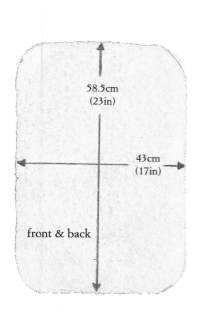

58.5cm
(23in)

43cm
(17in)

front & back

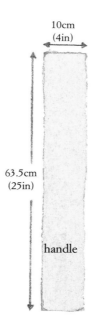

10cm
(4in)

63.5cm
(25in)

handle

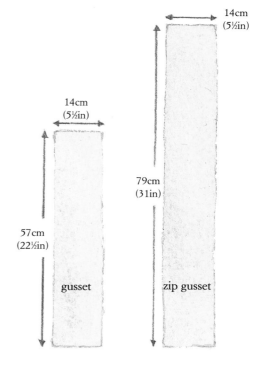

14cm
(5½in)

57cm
(22½in)

gusset

14cm
(5½in)

79cm
(31in)

zip gusset

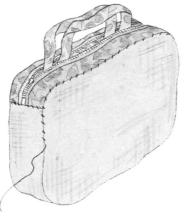

fig 3

To attach the gusset lining and complete
1 Turn under 1.5cm (⅝in) on both short ends of the gusset lining and press.
2 With the right sides of the gusset lining and the front lining facing, sandwich the front piece between the two. Pin, tack and stitch the gusset lining to the front of the bag. Press the seam towards the gusset. On the zip gusset, the seam should disappear under the folded edge. Slip stitch the folded edge down.
3 Bring the gusset lining over the gusset and slip stitch the long folded edge on to the stitching of the other gusset seam with neat stitches (fig 3).
4 Slip stitch the short folded edge on to the zip gusset. Open the zip and turn the bag right side out.

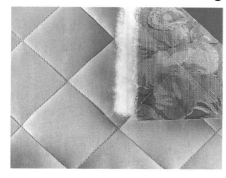

Quilting

Quilting is traditionally used to add warmth to fabrics. Wadding is sandwiched between two layers of fabric which are then stitched together, either by hand or machine. The stitching can be be worked either in straight lines or made into a feature following intricate patterns, which look especially effective on plain fabrics.

Quilted fabric is also protective and strong, making it especially suitable for bags. Vertical lines of topstitching can be applied to decorate either bag.

1 Mark evenly spaced lines across the bag about 2.5–5cm (1–2in) apart.
2 Place the wadding between the fabric and the lining, tack firmly together from the centre out to the edges.
3 Stitch along the marked lines using matching, or contrasting thread.
4 Measure and mark the horizontal quilting lines and stitch in the same way to complete.

bench cushion

Outdoor living is becoming increasingly popular, and a cushioned garden bench makes life much more comfortable. Once the art of gusset making has been mastered, box cushions are not difficult to construct. Choose a strong, hardwearing fabric that can weather the sunlight and light summer showers when stitched around a foam cushion. The extra-long zip will help to ease the cover off the cushion, making it easy to launder.

You will need

Paper for patterns
Fabric (see To cut out, below)
Matching sewing thread
Fabric for piping
Zip, equal in length to back edge of
  cushion plus 20cm (8in)
Foam cushion pad, cut to required size

To cut out

1 Measure the cushion pad and draw up a paper pattern for the top and base sections, adding twice the seam allowance to the length and width.
2 Make a paper pattern for the zip gusset, the same length as the zip plus twice the seam allowance x the depth of the cushion pad plus twice the seam allowance. Make a paper pattern for the remaining gusset section by measuring the remaining length around the cushion and adding twice the seam allowance all round. It may be necessary to join 2 pieces together to gain the required length.
3 Prepare the main fabric by straightening the cut edge so that it is at right angles to the selvedges.
4 Place the cushion top pattern piece on the main fabric, making sure that any printed design is centralized and that the long side lies parallel to the newly cut edge of the fabric. Pin in position. Repeat with the base pattern piece.
5 Fit the gusset pattern pieces on to the fabric. They can lie either along or across the grain of the fabric, depending on the effect required, but you must be consistent in the way you place them. Cut out all the pattern pieces. Cut out a second zip gusset piece.

To make and insert the piping

1 From the piping fabric cut out bias strips 3cm (1¼in) wide and join them into one length twice the circumference of the cushion pad, plus extra for joining. Fold the piping lengthways with wrong sides together and tack.
2 With cut edges together and starting at the centre of the back edge, pin the piping in place around the cushion top. Tack up to the first corner.
3 Using sharp scissors, clip the piping to allow it to turn the corner – the clip will open into a right angle (fig 1).
4 Continue to tack the piping on to the cushion top, snipping all the corners in the same way. When you reach the join, stitch the piping strip together to fit.
5 Repeat steps 1–4 on the cushion base.

To make the gusset

1 With wrong sides together, fold each zip gusset in half lengthways with wrong sides together. Tack the long edges together. Press.
2 Sew the zip centrally in between the folded edges of each zip gusset (fig 2).
3 With right sides together, join the gusset pieces into a ring. Partially open the zip.

To make up

1 With right sides together, join the gusset to the top (fig 3) and base sections, clipping the gusset at the corners – each clip should open into a right angle at each corner. Stitch the gusset in place.
2 Turn the cushion cover right side out and open the zip fully. Insert the cushion pad and close the zip.

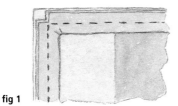

fig 1

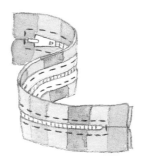

fig 2

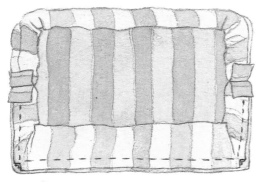

fig 3

wrap-around skirt

This free-flowing skirt made up in polyester will pack into a tiny space in a holdall and still come out looking as good as new – a definite must for a holiday wardrobe. The wrap-around style and flattering tie fastening will accommodate all shapes and sizes, and as it is quick to stitch you can run up several skirts in different fabrics, from brightly coloured cottons to fine, plain wools.

You will need
2m (2¼yd) polyester fabric, 115cm (45in) wide
Matching sewing thread

To scale up the patterns
Draw up the patterns using the measurements shown on the shapes below. Alternatively, turn to page 98 and scale up the patterns from the diagrams.

To cut out
1 back
1 left front
1 right front
1 right front facing
1 left front facing
1 back facing
2 ties 84 x 7cm (33 x 3in)

To make the tie
Place tie pieces with right sides together. Trim one end of tie pieces into a point. Pin, tack and stitch 1.3cm (½in) from the long cut edges and across pointed end. Turn right side out and press.

To make up
1 Stitch the darts in the back piece and press them towards the centre back.
2 Join the side seams, leaving a 2.5cm (1in) opening 2cm (¾in) from the top edge on the right-hand side seam (fig 1, right). Neaten; press the seams open.
3 Join the side seams on the facings, leaving a 2.5cm (1in) opening 2cm (¾in) from the top edge on the right-hand side seam. Press the seams open. Turn in 6mm (¼in) along the bottom edge of the facing and machine stitch.

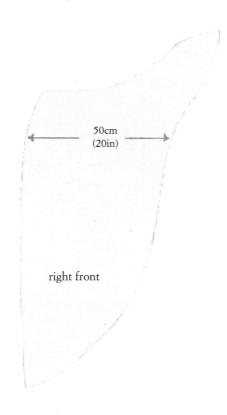

50cm
(20in)

right front

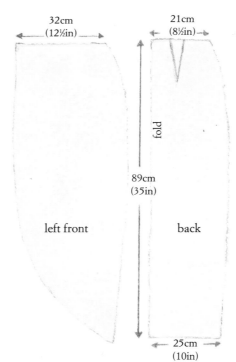

32cm
(12½in)

21cm
(8½in)

fold

89cm
(35in)

left front

back

25cm
(10in)

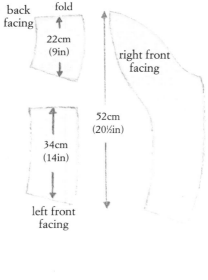

back facing

fold

22cm
(9in)

right front facing

52cm
(20½in)

34cm
(14in)

left front facing

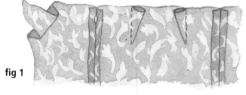

fig 1

fig 2

fig 3

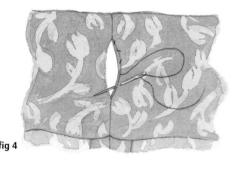

fig 4

4 With cut edges matching, pin, tack and stitch the tie in place on the right side of the left-hand front piece (fig 2).

5 With right sides together, pin the facing in position on the skirt, matching the cut edges along the waist, down the front and around the short tie (fig 3). Match the side seams on skirt and facing.

6 Tack and stitch the facing in place and press. Trim the seam and clip around the curves. Turn the facing to the wrong side and press. Catch the facing hem to each seam allowance with a few hand stitches.

7 Match up the gaps left in the skirt and facing seams. Slip stitch the folded edge of the facing seam to the folded edge of skirt seam around the opening (fig 4).

8 Make a 6mm (¼in) hem around the front and along the bottom of the skirt. Slip stitch in place.

47

Gathers, pleats & tucks

Pleats, tucks, darts, gathers and casings are all designed to take in fullness and reduce the width of a piece of fabric. Skirts and trousers can be full over the hips and, by using one of these methods, can also fit neatly into the waist; curtains can be made to fit a curtain track and hang in luxurious folds. Used skilfully and imaginatively, these techniques will add style and interest to a garment or project, as well as being functional.

One of the most dramatic ways to pleat the top of a curtain is to use triple pleats, and these are shown to great effect on the door curtain in this chapter. The loose-fitting trousers demonstrate one of the simplest methods of pulling in fullness – with a drawstring casing. In the shirts, fullness is taken up by the yoke and again at the cuff, while tucks have taken on a purely decorative role in the jewellery pouch.

Once you have perfected these methods, you can use your new-found skills in a variety of ways on garments and home furnishings.

gathers &
tucks

Gathering is one of the simplest ways of taking in fullness. Extra fullness is drawn up to the required length by pulling up a running stitch, and this method can be used on skirts at the waist, on sleeves at the head or cuff, on yokes or to make frills. To look professional, gathers must be made with care. They need to be distributed evenly and stroked down individually with a pin to make them lie neatly and in an orderly fashion.

Tucks control fullness in a precise way – each one needs to be accurately measured, pinned and stitched, to achieve a neat result. Tucks can also be used in a purely decorative way.

Making gathers

Gathering can be done by hand with a simple running stitch, or by machine using a large straight stitch and a loose tension, or by using a ruffler attachment.

By hand

The thread for gathering needs to be strong so that it can be pulled up without breaking.

1 Cut a piece of thread 10cm (4in) longer than the length to be gathered. This may be much longer than you are used to working with, but it is essential not to have joins.

2 Secure the thread. Work two rows of small running stitches approximately 6mm (¼in) apart, one above and one below the seamline (fig 1). The stitches should lie exactly above each other. Avoid gathering over a seam; instead, stop and start again on either side.

3 When you get to the end, do not finish off the threads but leave them hanging

until you are ready to pull them up.

4 Divide the gathered edge into an equal number of sections and mark with pins. Take the other piece to be joined to the gathers and divide into matching sections marking the divisions with pins.

5 Place the flat piece of fabric right side up and position the gathered piece on top, with the cut edges matching. Pin the two pieces of fabric together at the marked points. The pins should be placed at right angles to the cut edges and positioned so as not to interfere with pulling up the threads.

6 Hold the two gathering threads together and pull up until the piece of fabric measures the same length as the ungathered piece. Anchor the ends of the threads by twisting them around a pin in a figure-of-eight movement.

7 Arrange the gathers evenly. Put in more pins, then tack and machine stitch along the seamline.

8 Remove the gathering and tacking threads. Turn to the right side and stroke down the gathers with a pin.

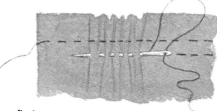

fig 1

By machine

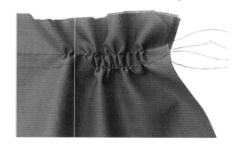

The basic method for making gathers by machine is the same as by hand, apart from the following points:

• Before making the two rows of gathering stitches, loosen the upper tension of the machine slightly and select the longest stitch length.

• Pull up the bobbin threads together from both ends (fig 2), and anchor on pins at both ends.

fig 2

pull up bobbin threads

Casings and drawstrings

A casing is one of the simplest ways in which to control fullness. It consists of a channel made in the fabric through which a piece of elastic, cord or ribbon is threaded and then pulled up to the required length. Casings have the advantage of being adjustable; they can also be used on curtains, where a pole can be threaded through the casing to gather up the fullness.

Elastic casing

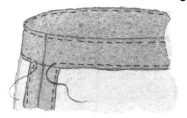

fig 3

An elastic casing is not quite as adjustable as a drawstring, because the elastic is stitched to a fixed length.

1 Fold over the edge of the fabric along the fitting line and tack the folded edge. Tuck under the cut edge and tack.

2 Stitch along the top of the casing and again along the fold at the lower edge of the casing, leaving a gap in the stitching (fig 3) through which to thread the elastic. Position the gap over a seam.

3 Fasten a safety pin to one end of the elastic and feed it around the casing. Overlap the ends of the elastic for 2cm (¾in) and stitch them together firmly; stitch the gap closed.

Drawstring casing

A drawstring casing is made in the same way as an elastic casing, but an opening must be left through which the drawstring can emerge. The simplest way to do this is to leave an opening in a seam. The other way is to make eyelets or buttonholes in the casing fabric before the casing itself is formed.

Tucks

Tucks are an attractive way of controlling fullness, but can also be used purely as decoration. They can be made on the right or wrong side of the fabric, but it is more usual for them to show on the right side. In addition, tucks can be stitched along their whole length or only part of the way, releasing the fullness where the stitching stops.

Tucks are usually grouped together; their width, and the spacing between them, can be varied to produce a range of different effects.

Tucks are made on the straight grain of the fabric. The folds and stitching must be exactly parallel and great care must be taken to ensure accuracy.

Pintucks are simply tiny tucks stitched very close to the folds. They can also be made quite successfully on the sewing machine using a specialist foot and twin needle.

1 Fold the fabric along the straight grain, with wrong sides together.

2 Measure the required width of the tuck from the fold and tack along this line through both layers of fabric (fig 4), checking the measurement as you go. Measure and tack all the tucks.

3 Stitch all the tucks along the tacking lines. The quilting guide on your machine can help to make the stitching lines exactly parallel to the folds. Make sure that you stitch all the tucks from the same side, so that the top thread of the machine is uppermost when the tucks are pressed to one side.

4 Remove the tacking. Press the stitching, and then press the tucks to one side (fig 5) .

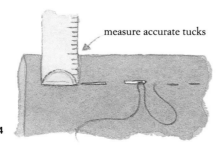

measure accurate tucks

fig 4

fig 5

drawstring trousers

Simple drawstring trousers are extremely comfortable to wear, as the combination of elastic and drawstring ties can be adjusted to fit any size of waist. These are made in sandwash silk, for a look that is both casual and smart. You can make up the same pattern in another fabric to create a completely different effect.

You will need
2.5m (3yd) silk, 115cm (45in) wide
Matching sewing thread
1.5m (1¾yd) elastic, 1cm (⅜in) wide
Small square fusible interfacing

To scale up the patterns
Draw up the patterns using the measurements shown on the shapes on page 54. Alternatively, turn to page 100 and scale up the patterns from the diagrams illustrated.

To cut out
2 trouser backs
2 trouser fronts
4 pockets
2 waistbands

To attach the pockets and join the outside legs
1 Lay the front leg pieces right side up on a flat surface. Place a pocket piece right side down on top of each leg piece, with the side edges matching and the top edge of the pocket matching the top edge of the leg piece.

2 Pin and tack the edge of the pocket piece on to the side edge of the leg piece, then stitch in place 6mm (¼in) from the edge (fig 1). Neaten and press the seam towards the pocket. The pocket piece should now stick out at the outside edge of the leg piece (fig 2). Repeat, to stitch the pocket pieces to the back trouser pieces.

fig 1

fig 2

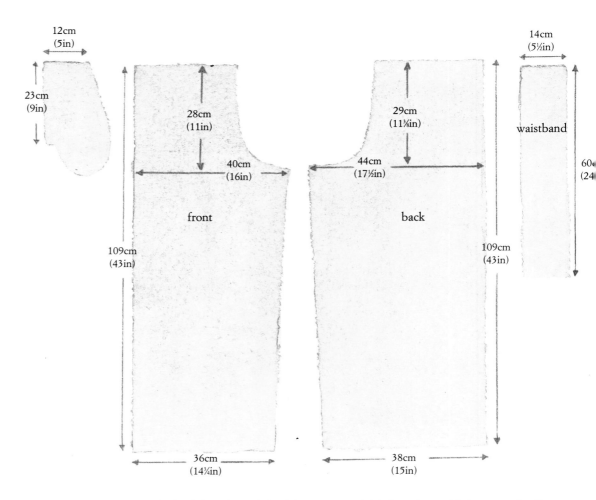

12cm
(5in)

23cm
(9in)

28cm
(11in)

40cm
(16in)

front

109cm
(43in)

36cm
(14¾in)

29cm
(11⅜in)

44cm
(17½in)

back

109cm
(43in)

38cm
(15in)

14cm
(5½in)

waistband

60
(24

3 Lay the back leg pieces right side up on a flat surface. Place the front leg pieces right side down on top of the back leg pieces, matching up the cut edges of the outside legs and the pockets. Pin and tack these pieces together.

4 Stitch each outside leg seam for 5cm (2in) down from the top, then leave an opening of 15cm (6in), and continue stitching to the bottom of the leg (fig 3).
5 Stitch round the pockets, joining the stitching to side-seam stitching (fig 4).
6 Clip the seam below the pockets to allow you to press it towards the front of the trousers. Neaten the seam, then tack the upper edge of the pocket to the top of the trousers.

To join the inside legs
1 Match up the cut edges of each inside leg. Pin and tack: the back leg pieces are bigger than the fronts and therefore will no longer lie flat.
2 Starting at the top, stitch and neaten these seams. Press.

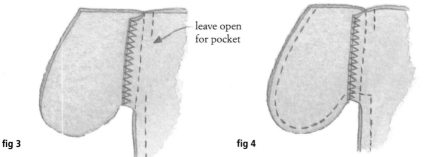

leave open
for pocket

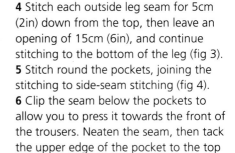

fig 3

fig 4

To join the crotch

1 With right sides facing and the crotch seams matching, place one leg inside the other. Pin and tack the crotch (fig 5).

2 Stitch the crotch seam and reinforce with a second row of stitching.

3 Trim the seam on either side of the inside leg seam for about 15cm (6in) and overlock or oversew the cut edges together. Clip the seam above this point to allow you to press open the upper part. Neaten the seam.

To make and join on the waistband

1 Iron a small square of interfacing behind the eyelet positions and work 2 eyelets or buttonholes by hand or machine (fig 6).

2 Pin and tack the ends of the waistband together to form a circle. At one side, stitch 1.5cm (⅝in), then leave an opening of 4cm (1½in) and stitch to the end (fig 7). Leave the tacking in place.

3 With right sides together, place the waistband on the trousers at the waist, matching the waistband seams to the side seams. Pin, tack and stitch the waistband in place (fig 8), then press the seam towards the waistband and trim.

4 Turn the waistband to the wrong side of the trousers and turn under the seam allowance on the cut edge. Pin this folded edge on to the first line of stitching and slip stitch in place. Press the waistband, paying particular attention to the folded edge at the top.

5 Make a row of machine stitches 1.5cm (⅝in) down from and parallel to the folded edge of the waistband, then make a second row of stitching 2.5cm (1in) down from and parallel to the other row, to make 3 channels.

6 Remove the earlier tacking and thread elastic through the top and bottom channels (fig 9). Join the elastic and slip stitch the openings closed.

fig 5

fig 6

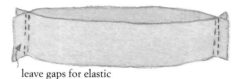

leave gaps for elastic

fig 7

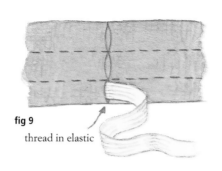

fig 8

fig 9

thread in elastic

To make the tie

1 Cut a tie strip 200 x 4cm (80 x 1½). Fold the tie strip in half lengthways with right sides together and machine stitch 6mm (¼in) from the long cut edge. Trim the seam and turn the tie right side out. Tuck in the ends and slip stitch.

2 Thread the tie through the centre channel and knot the ends.

To finish

Turn up 5cm (2in) hems at the bottom edges of the trouser legs, tuck under the cut edges. Pin, tack and slip stitch.

jewellery pouch

This jewellery pouch makes a delightful gift, but you will surely want to make one for yourself as well. The fabric used here is striped, and the pieces have been cut to make full use of this effect. However, the pouch is equally successful made up in a plain fabric – particularly silk, which catches the light so well. The surface decoration of pintucks makes an attractive finishing touch.

You will need

75cm (30in) fabric, 115cm (45in) wide
Matching sewing thread
40cm (16in) wadding, 90cm (36in) wide
Press stud

To cut out and prepare the pieces

1 Cut out the following pieces in fabric, adding 1.3cm (½in) for seam allowances unless otherwise specified:
Front 19 x 62.5cm (7½ x 25in)
Front facing 19 x 21cm (7½ x 8½in)
Back 19 x 21cm (7½ x 8½in)
Back facing 19 x 21cm (7½ x 8½in)
Leaf 28 x 18cm (11 x 7in)
Front pocket 16.5 x 14.5cm (6½ x 5¾in)
Back pocket 21 x 17cm (8½ x 6¾in)
Flap 9 x 21cm (3½ x 8½in)
Ties (2) 28 x 2.5cm (11 x 1in), plus 6mm (¼in) seam allowance
Roll 15 x 5cm (6 x 2in), plus 6mm (¼in) seam allowance
2 Cut out 2 pieces of wadding, one 18 x 14cm (7 x 5½in) and the other 34 x 21cm (14 x 8½in).

To make the tucks

1 Make 6mm (¼in) tucks parallel with the long edges across the front piece. Press all the tucks in one direction. From this tucked piece, cut out a rectangle 19 x 21cm (7½ x 8½in).
2 Work a row of stitching parallel to and 1cm (⅜in) away from the edge along and through the tucks in the direction in which they have been pressed. Work another row of stitching 11cm (4½in) from the same edge, keeping the tucks lying in the same direction.
3 Making the tucks lie in the opposite direction, work 2 more parallel rows of stitching, 1cm (⅜in) and 11cm (4½in) away from the opposite edge.
4 Join the front and back pieces along one long side. Trim the seam and press.

To make and attach the pockets

1 Make a double 1.3cm (½in) hem at the top of the front pocket piece. Pin, tack and stitch in place. Turn under 1.3cm (½in) on the remaining 3 sides and press.
2 Place the pocket, right side up, in position on the front facing, an equal distance from each side edge and 2.5cm (1in) from the bottom edge. Pin, tack and stitch it in position, working a small triangle at either side of the top of the pocket (fig 1).
3 Make a hem along one of the long sides of the back pocket piece in the same way as for the front pocket. Make a similar hem along one of the long sides of the flap piece.
4 Place the pocket piece on top of the back facing with cut edges together. Place the flap on top, with the hem overlapping the pocket hem and the cut edges matching the facing (fig 2). Pin, tack and stitch together, 6mm (¼in) away from the cut edge.

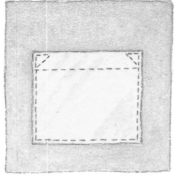

fig 1

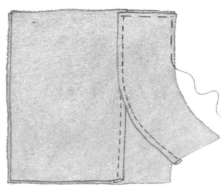

fig 2

To make and attach the leaf

1 Fold the leaf piece in half widthways with right sides together. Place a piece of wadding behind, then pin, tack and stitch along the 2 short edges (fig 3). Trim the seam, then turn right side out and press.

2 Place the leaf on top of the front facing, with the cut edges matching the cut edges on the right side of the facing and an equal distance from the top and bottom.

3 With right sides together and edges matching, place the back facing (plus pocket) on top of the front facing with the leaf sandwiched in between. Pin, tack and stitch this one edge together (fig 4). Trim the seam and press.

To make and attach the roll

1 Fold the roll piece in half lengthways with right sides together and stitch 6mm (¼in) from the long cut edge and across one end. Turn right side out and stuff with offcuts of wadding. Turn in the ends and slip stitch.

2 Stitch one side of a press stud to one end of the roll. Place the roll on the front facing between the top of the pocket and the top edge of the facing.

3 Stitch one end of the roll on to the facing, then stitch the other half of the press stud on to the facing to match up with the stud on the roll.

To make and attach the ties

1 Fold the tie pieces in half lengthways with right sides together and stitch 6mm (¼in) from the long cut edge. Turn right side out.

2 Tack the ties in place half-way down the pouch, one on the right and one on the left side of the facing (fig 5).

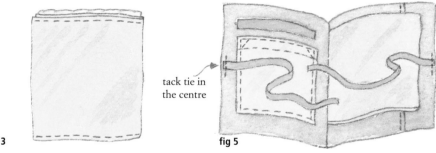

tack tie in the centre

fig 3

fig 5

fig 4

To make up

1 With right sides together, place the front and back pieces on top of the facings, sandwiching the ties in between. Pin and tack in place.

2 Place the wadding pieces on top of these pieces and tack in place. Stitch through all layers 1.3cm (½in) from the edge all the way round, leaving a gap of about 7cm (3in) for turning. Turn the pouch right side out and press. Slip stitch the gap closed.

3 Tuck in cut edges of ties and slip stitch.

shirts

Shirts are always in fashion and make a welcome addition to any wardrobe. These cool shirts are made in linen and cotton. The plain version is made very simply with a pleat at the back, and the pattern is then adapted for the lawn shirt, with pintucks added for decoration and gathers replacing the pleat at the back.

Plain shirt

Clean-cut lines and cool linen fabric make this an ideal shirt. The smart, topstitched sleeve openings add to the tailored look. Wear it tucked into trousers or hanging free.

You will need
2.5m (3yd) linen, 115cm (45in) wide *or*
2m (2¼yd) linen, 150cm (60in) wide
Matching sewing thread
25cm (10in) interfacing, 90cm (36in)
   wide
11 buttons

To scale up the patterns
Draw up the patterns using the measurements shown on the shapes on page 63. Or, turn to page 102 and scale up the patterns from the diagrams.

To cut out
From fabric
1 back
2 back yokes
1 left front
1 right front
2 sleeves
2 collars
2 cuffs
2 plackets
From interfacing
1 collar
2 cuffs

To make the pleat
1 Mark the centre back. Measure and mark 2.5cm (1in) to either side. With the right side of the back piece facing, fold the marks to the centre back.

2 Press and tack across the pleat along the seamline (fig 1).

To make the back
1 With right sides together, pin and tack a yoke on to the upper edge of back.
2 Place the right side of the second yoke piece (the yoke facing) to the wrong side of the back piece. Pin, tack and stitch through all layers, sandwiching the back between the 2 yoke pieces (fig 2). Press the seam towards the yoke.
3 Make a 6mm (¼in) double hem on the lower edge of back and stitch in place.

To make the front
1 On the right front piece, fold the buttonhole band to the right side along the fold lines. Pin, tack and stitch the band to the right side of the front.
2 On the left front piece, fold the band to the wrong side along the fold lines.
3 With right sides together, pin, tack and stitch the front edges of the yoke to the upper edge of the fronts. Press the seams towards the yoke.
4 Bring the yoke facing over to the front, turn under the seam allowance and slip stitch on to the machine stitching. Tack the yoke pieces together at the neck and shoulder edge.
5 Make a double 6mm (¼in) hem along the lower edge of the front and stitch.

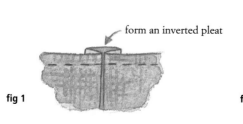

form an inverted pleat

fig 1

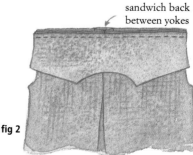

sandwich back between yokes

fig 2

fig 3

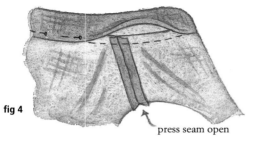

fig 4

press seam open

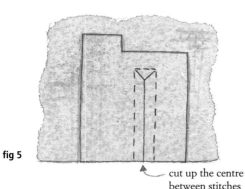

fig 5

cut up the centre
between stitches

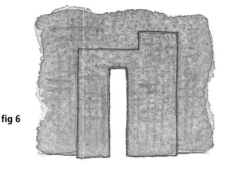

fig 6

To make and attach the collar

1 Pin and tack the collar interfacing to one collar piece.

2 Turn under the seam allowance along the lower edge of the remaining collar piece. Press and trim.

3 Right sides facing, pin, tack and stitch the collar pieces together, leaving the lower edge open (fig 3). Trim the seam and press. Turn right side out and press.

4 With right sides together, pin, tack and stitch the unfolded edge of the collar to the neck edge of the shirt. Press the seam towards the collar. Pin the remaining folded edge of the collar over the previous stitches; pin and tack (fig 4). Topstitch around the collar.

To make and set in the sleeves

1 For each sleeve, turn under a 1cm (⅜in) seam allowance along both the side edges and the short upper edge of the placket and press.

2 Place the right side of the placket to the wrong side of the sleeve, over the marked placket position. Make a rectangle of stitching 2 x 12cm (¾ x 5in), 4cm (1½in) from the shorter edge of the placket. Cut up the centre of this rectangle to within 6mm (¼in) of the top and clip into the corners close to the stitching (fig 5).

3 Turn the placket to the right side of the sleeve and press the seam towards the placket (fig 6).

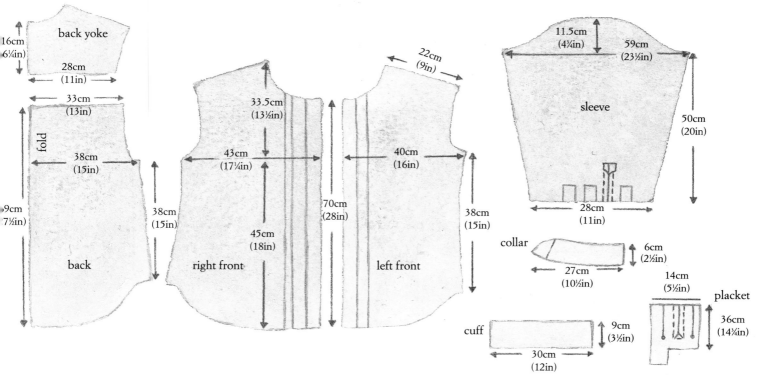

back yoke

16cm
6¼in)

28cm
(11in)

33cm
(13in)

fold

38cm
(15in)

9cm
7½in)

38cm
(15in)

back

33.5cm
(13½in)

43cm
(17¼in)

45cm
(18in)

70cm
(28in)

right front

22cm
(9in)

40cm
(16in)

38cm
(15in)

left front

11.5cm
(4¾in)

59cm
(23½in)

sleeve

50cm
(20in)

28cm
(11in)

collar

6cm
(2½in)

27cm
(10½in)

14cm
(5½in)

placket

36cm
(14¼in)

cuff

9cm
(3½in)

30cm
(12in)

4 Fold the shorter side of the placket in half lengthways over the seam and stitch in place (fig 7). Repeat with the longer side of the placket. Pin the upper edge of the placket to the sleeve and stitch in place (fig 8).

5 Make 3 pleats 1.5cm (⅝in) deep at the lower edge of the sleeve, one on the underside of the sleeve and 2 on the upper side, all facing the placket. Tack the pleats in place.

6 With right sides together, pin, tack and stitch the sleeve to the main body of the shirt. Press the seam towards the shoulder and topstitch.

7 Join the side seam of the main body from the hem through to the lower edge of the sleeve.

To make and attach the cuffs

1 For each cuff, pin and tack the cuff interfacing to the wrong side of the cuff piece. Fold the cuff in half lengthways with right sides together. Turn up, press and trim the seam allowance along one long edge of the cuff.

2 Stitch the short ends of the cuff together. Turn right side out and press.

3 Pin, tack and stitch the unfolded edge of the cuff to the right side of the sleeve. Trim the seam allowance and press the seam towards the cuff.

4 Slip stitch the folded edge of the cuff on to the machine stitching on the wrong side. Topstitch around the cuff.

To finish

Make buttonholes at equal distances down the front band, and on the cuffs and placket. Sew buttons on to the shirt to correspond with the buttonholes.

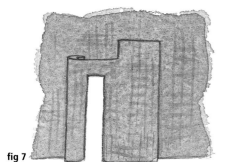

fig 7

fig 8

Pintucked shirt

A good finished result depends on the accuracy of the pintucks. Make sure that they are measured and stitched with care for a professional look.

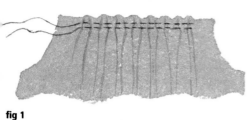

fig 1

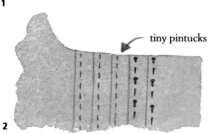

tiny pintucks

fig 2

You will need
2.5m (3yd) cotton lawn, 115cm (45in) wide *or*
2m (2¼yd) cotton lawn, 150cm (60in) wide
Matching sewing thread
25cm (10in) interfacing, 90cm (36in) wide
11 buttons

To scale up the patterns
Draw up the patterns using the measurements shown on the shapes below and on page 63. Alternatively, turn to page 102 and scale up the patterns from the diagrams.

To cut out
From fabric
1 back
2 back yokes
2 fronts
2 sleeves
2 collars
2 cuffs
2 plackets

From interfacing
1 collar
2 cuffs

To make the back
1 Gather the upper edge of the back piece 15cm (6in) in from either side and pull up the gathers to match the lower edge of the yoke (fig 1). With right sides together, pin and tack a yoke piece on to the gathered upper edge of the back.
2 Follow steps 2 and 3 of the back instructions for the Plain Shirt.

To make the front
1 Make 5 pintucks, each 6mm (¼in) wide and 1cm (⅜in) apart, down the front of the shirt, starting 13cm (5¼in) from the edge (fig 2).
2 Follow steps 1–5 of the front instructions for the Plain Shirt.

To complete
To make and attach the collar, sleeves, cuffs, buttonholes and buttons, follow the instructions for the Plain Shirt.

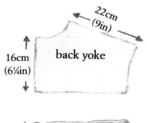

22cm (9in)

16cm (6¼in)   back yoke

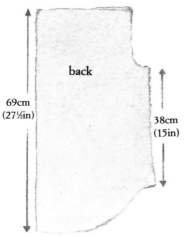

back

69cm (27½in)

38cm (15in)

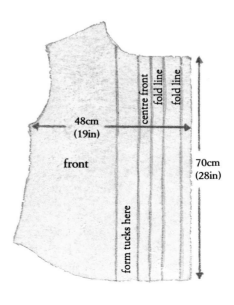

48cm (19in)

centre front

fold line

fold line

front

70cm (28in)

form tucks here

65

pleats

At their simplest, pleats are folds of fabric taken in wherever fullness needs to be controlled. Successful pleats do rely on careful measuring, marking, and stitching.

Pleats are sometimes formed and then attached to another, shorter piece of fabric with a seam. If the pleats are then allowed to fall softly without further stitching they are called unpressed pleats. For a more structured style, the pleats can be pressed down their full length. To help keep pleats in shape, they can be stitched part of the way down the folds. On curtains, pleats are not normally enclosed in a seam, but are formed on the neatened edge of the curtain and then partially stitched down to keep them in place.

There are several types of pleats including knife, box and inverted pleats, which are used mainly in garments, and cartridge, goblet and triple pleats, which are used almost exclusively in curtains and soft furnishing projects.

Raised pleats

These pleats do not lie flat but stand proud of the fabric. They are not suitable for garment making and are used almost exclusively for curtain headings.

Special tapes are available which can be attached to the fabric so that when the cords are pulled, pleats are formed. However, a more satisfactory and elegant finish is achieved by pleating by hand. Although a lot more work and skill is involved, the superior quality of the finished result is definitely worth the extra effort.

To estimate the fabric required for a hand-pleated heading, allow for 2–2½ times the width of the track. A length of buckram – a 12cm (5in) deep heavyweight stiffening strip – is enclosed across the top of the curtain before the hand pleats are formed to give them extra body and shape.

Cartridge pleats

Cartridge pleats are small round pleats spaced at regular intervals along the top of a curtain. The cylindrical forms are filled with rolled-up heavyweight interfacing to help keep the rounded shape.

1 Measure and mark the positions of the pleats. Generally, cartridge pleats need about 9cm (3½in) of fabric to form each pleat. Space the pleats about 12cm (5in) apart across the fabric.
2 Fold the pleats along the top edge of the fabric with wrong sides together, making sure that the top edges are lined up and the pleat markings match. Pin the pleats into position.

3 Stitch exactly parallel to the folded edges of the pleats, from the top edge to 1.5cm (⅝in) below the edge of the buckram (fig 1).
4 Form each pleat into a round cylinder. Cut a piece of interfacing to the depth of the pleat and the circumference of the cylinder. Roll up the interfacing and slide it into the pleat (fig 2) to help retain its rounded shape.

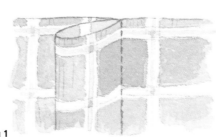

fig 1

fig 2

Goblet pleats

Goblet pleats are made in the same way as cartridge pleats, but they are larger single pleats. The bottom of each pleat is drawn in and secured, and the pleat is then stuffed to give a good rounded shape. The finished effect is very grand and elegant, so these pleats are best used on long curtains where a formal look is required. Once made, curtains with goblet pleats do not draw back easily, so are best left drawn across the window and draped open with tie backs.

1 Measure and mark the positions of the pleats. Generally goblet pleats need 14cm (5½in) of fabric to form each pleat. Space the pleats 14cm (5½in) apart.
2 Form the basic pleats as for cartridge pleats steps 2 and 3 (fig 3).

3 Draw in the base of each pleat very tightly and stitch securely with strong thread, moulding the upper part of the pleat into a cup or goblet shape (fig 4).
4 Stuff the goblet with wadding to give a good rounded shape.

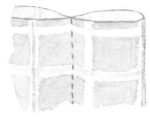

fig 3

fig 4

Box pleats

Unlike cartridge and goblet pleats, which stand proud, box pleats lie flat. They are suitable for both soft furnishings and garment making, and can be enclosed in a supporting band or formed after the top edge is finished. Sometimes they are allowed to hang free and loose, sometimes they are part sewn down their length for a more formal effect. For tailored pleats, they can be pressed down their full length and held together at the base with a bar tack.

1 Prepare the top edge if necessary. Measure and mark the positions of the pleats. For pleats 5cm (2in) wide, mark 10cm (4in) pleats and 10cm (4in) spaces across the whole top edge.
2 Form the basic pleats as for cartridge pleats steps 2 and 3 (fig 5).
3 Fold the pleats flat, with the stitching

line to the centre so that there is the same amount of pleat on either side (fig 6). Press and tack down.
4 If the pleats are to be sewn to a supporting band, stitch this on now; otherwise, catch stitch the pleats permanently in position by hand to the depth of the machine stitching.

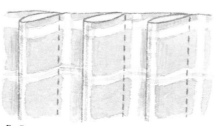

fig 5

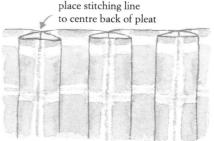

place stitching line to centre back of pleat

fig 6

curtain call

Layering a sheer fabric over a heavy linen gives the right thickness for a door curtain without it appearing too heavy and unyielding. The bound edge keeps the two fabrics anchored together, while the top is hand stitched with handsome triple pleats. Let the curtain hang straight, with a longer length puddling over the floor, or catch it back to one side in an attractive sweep of fabric.

You will need

Plain linen (see To cut out, below)
Sheer check cotton, (see To cut out, below)
Buckram, 12cm (5in) deep, length equal to width of unpleated curtain
Matching sewing threads
Curtain hooks

To cut out

1 Measure the width of the door and add 18cm (7in) for each pleat. Cut out as many widths of linen and of sheer fabric as necessary, so that when joined they will equal the required width including pleat allowances.
2 For the top facing, from plain linen cut out the same number of fabric widths as for the main curtain, each 26cm (10¼in) deep.
3 For binding the outer edge, cut out 2 pieces of plain linen each 9cm (3½in) wide x the curtain length plus 6cm (2½in) for seam allowances, and 1 piece 9cm (3½in) wide x the curtain width plus 9cm (3½in) for seam allowances.

To make up

1 Join the fabric widths together with machine-felled seams to make one piece. Repeat to make up one piece in sheer fabric. Lay out the linen curtain right side up, then lay the sheer curtain right side up over the top. Pin and tack the curtains together, matching any seams.
2 Seam the facing lengths together with plain, flat seams. With right sides together and matching seams, place the facing to the top of the curtain; pin, tack and stitch in place. Trim the seam, then fold down the facing and press with the seam to the edge.
3 Position the buckram between the curtain and the facing. Tuck the bottom edge of the facing up and under the buckram to enclose it, and pin in place.
4 Measure and mark positions for pleats 18cm (7in) wide, spacing them approximately 12cm (5in) apart, evenly along the top edge of the curtain. Create a triple pleat at each mark.
5 Fold in the top edge of the fabric with the wrong sides together, making sure that the top edges are lined up and that the pleat markings match. Pin the pleats into position.
7 Stitch exactly parallel to the folded edges of the pleats, from the top edge to 1.5cm (⅝in) below the edge of the buckram (fig 1).
8 Take hold of a pleat between your finger and thumb at the folded edge and push it back to the line of stitching. Another 2 pleats should stick out at either side of your finger and thumb; these 3 pleats should all be the same size. Crease these 3 pleats along their length.
9 Oversew neatly across the bottom of each pleat, then oversew at the top of the pleat where the folds meet the machine stitching (fig 2).

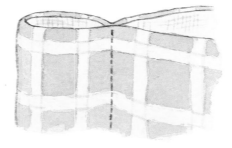

fig 1

fig 2

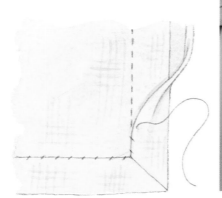

fig 3

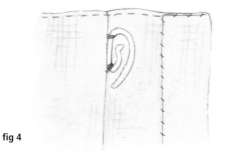

fig 4

To make and attach the binding

1 Fold the binding in half lengthways with wrong sides facing and press. At one end of each side binding, fold up the cut edges to match the folded edge and press. Unfold and cut along the pressed line. Repeat to cut diagonally across both ends of the base binding.

2 With the binding unfolded, place the mitred edges with right sides facing; pin, tack and stitch them together to within 1.5cm (⅝in) of the cut edges. Trim and press the seams to the edge. Refold the binding in half and press.

3 Place one edge of the binding to the curtain with right sides together and seam line of binding 3cm (1¼in) in from the outer edge of the curtain. Match the mitred seams to the base corners of the curtain. Pin, tack and stitch the binding to the curtain. At the base corners the binding will fan out to create a neat corner.

4 Tuck under the remaining cut edge of the binding on the wrong side of the curtain and slip stitch it by hand to the previous stitches on the wrong side (fig 3). Press.

To finish

1 At the top edge, tuck under the cut edges of the binding to match the top edge of the curtain and slip stitch in place as before.

2 Hand sew curtain hooks to the wrong side of the curtain, 4cm (1½in) down from the top edge. Sew a hook behind each pleat position (fig 4).

3 Give the curtain a final press and hang from a curtain pole or track.

Finishes, fastenings
& edgings

Using distinctive trimmings adds the final flourish to your sewing projects. Whether you weave fantasies with tassels and fringing or add a smart bound edge, it is clever details which lift the homemade into the world of the professional sewer.

Decorative trimmings emphasize exuberant fabrics and provide a rich contribution to the presentation of your sewing skills. On these pages you will discover how to add a creative touch with confidence and imagination. Choose inventive ways to fasten cushions and clothes, bring a touch of pompon fun to a colourful pelmet, and twist and turn tape into intricate flower designs.

rouleau & loops

Rouleau is a narrow tube made from fabric cut out on the true cross, seamed and turned to the right side. It can vary in thickness according to its use and the chosen fabric. The rouleau can either be made flat by trimming down the seam allowances, or fat and round by leaving the seam allowances to add bulk inside the tubing.

Once made up, rouleau has many uses. They make shoestring straps for camisoles and lingerie, can be plaited together as an attractive trimming, and may be used as ties and decorative bows, but their most popular use is for button loops. If you are making a lot of rouleau it is worth buying a rouleau turner, which makes life a lot easier.

Rouleau

To make a firm rounded tube, pad the rouleau with its own seam allowance, which instead of being trimmed off is turned to the inside.

1 Cut out a strip of fabric on the true cross to the finished length and four times the finished width required.
2 With right sides together, fold the tube in half lengthways. Stitch down the strip, stretching the fabric as you go.
3 If you have a rouleau turner, use it to turn the tube the right way out. If not, tie the threads from the machine stitching to a large-eyed blunt needle (fig 1) and use this to pull the tube the right way out (fig 2).

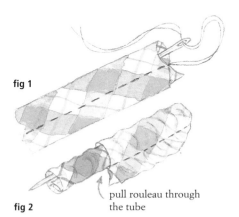

fig 1

fig 2

pull rouleau through
the tube

Corded rouleau

Rouleau is much stronger and rounder if it is fitted with a cord. Any width of fine cord or piping cord can be used. If the fabric is very fine, it is best to use it double or line it with another fabric so that the ridges of the cord are not so prominent.

1 Cut out a strip of fabric on the true cross in the same way as for rouleau, above.
2 Cut a piece of cord of the desired thickness and twice as long as the rouleau. Find the centre of the cord and place it on the right side of the end of the fabric strip.

3 Fold the fabric strip around the cord, stitch across the strip through the cord to anchor the strip (fig 3) and secure it by stitching close to the cord using the zip or piping foot.
4 Pull the fabric tube back over the other half of the cord (fig 4) and cut off the excess cord.

fig 3

fig 4

Button loops

Button loops extending beyond the fabric opening make an attractive alternative to buttonholes. Tiny loops look delicate on fine fabrics for lingerie or evening wear, while larger loops can be used on jackets or to fasten cushion covers. The loops can vary greatly in thickness and size depending on their use, the fabric and the design of the article, and may be either hidden or on show. Loops can be made from rouleau, corded rouleau, cord, fine tape or braid.

A single loop

A single loop can be used on a tailored jacket in place of a buttonhole, and is generally bigger and thicker than the loops in a row. A single loop is usually attached to an edge without the need for a paper guide. Position and sew the single loop in place, and neaten with a facing.

1 Make up a short length of rouleau. Form into a single loop and pin on to the right side of the item at the marked position (fig 5), with the ends to the cut edge and the loop facing inwards.
2 Stitch along the seamline and then attach the facing.

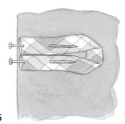

fig 5

Row of loops

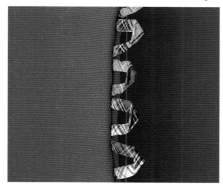

A row of loops fitted together down the front or back of the bodice of a ballgown or wedding dress, with self-covered ball buttons, looks very attractive. Alternatively, space out the loops or group them in twos or threes with a space between the groups. They are also very pleasing on a wide cuff or cummerbund.

1 Make up a very narrow rouleau, about three times as long as the opening along which the row of loops will fit.
2 Take a piece of stiff paper the same length as the opening and mark out the size and spacing of the loops. Mark in the seamline.
3 Pin the rouleau on to the paper and then stitch through the rouleau and the

paper along the seamline (fig 6).
4 Place the paper with the rouleau in position on the right side of the fabric, with the rouleau uppermost. Match the seamlines.
5 Stitch the paper and rouleau to the fabric over the stitching, following the marked lines (fig 7). Tear away the paper. Neaten with a facing (fig 8).

fig 6

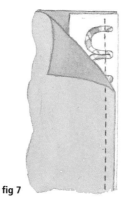

fig 7

fig 8

75

finishing

A very narrow hand-rolled hem is the most professional way to finish the edge of very fine fabrics such as fine silks, chiffon and georgette, and is certainly the best choice for the edges of a silk scarf.

Binding is another neat way of finishing an edge. The binding can match the fabric or be a complete contrast, and the width may vary from very narrow to quite wide, depending on the project and the fabric being used.

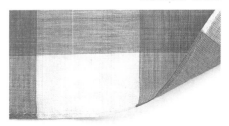

Rolled hem

This is quite a difficult process to master, but with a little time and patience it can be done and the result, although time consuming, is well worth the effort. If you have difficulty in getting the roll started, it is sometimes helpful to make a row of machine stitching near the edge of the fabric and then trim close to it. This gives stability to the edge and makes the rolling easier.

1 Cut a neat edge to the fabric. If it frays easily, it is advisable to trim as you sew.
2 With the wrong side of the fabric facing, use the finger and thumb of your left hand to roll a tiny hem towards you. This may take a little practice.
3 Thread a needle with good-quality silk thread and pick up one fabric thread under the roll and another thread on the main fabric (fig 1).

4 Continue in this manner, rolling the fabric with the left hand and stitching with the right.

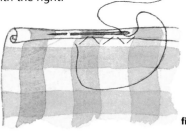

fig 1

Bound edge

The colour and width of a bound edge can be chosen to suit an individual project perfectly. For example, silk underwear would require a very narrow binding, probably in a matching colour, while at the opposite end of the spectrum a quilted bedspread would need quite a wide binding, probably in a contrasting colour.

If the edge to be bound is completely straight, the binding can be cut on the straight grain of the fabric, but if there are curves, cut the binding on the cross grain.

1 Cut out the strips for the binding on either the straight or cross grain and to the length required. The width of the strips should be twice the required finished width plus twice the seam allowance.
2 Place the edge of the binding against the edge of the fabric, with right sides together. Pin, tack and stitch the binding

in place (fig 2).
3 Fold the binding over the edge to the wrong side of the fabric. Turn under the cut edge of the binding and butt this fold up against the machine stitching. Pin and tack in position.
4 Slip stitch into the line of machine stitches (fig 3). Press carefully along the binding edge.

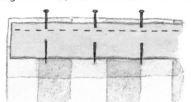

fig 2

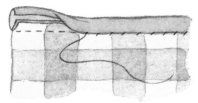

fig 3

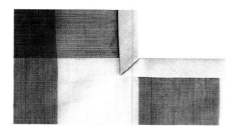

Inside corners

1 Reinforce and clip the corner.
2 With right sides together, stitch the binding to the edge of the fabric, pivoting on the machine needle at the corner and continuing to the end (fig 4).

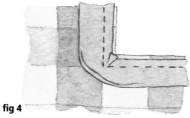

fig 4

3 Make a mitre in the binding on the right side, then turn over the work and repeat on the other side.
4 Slip stitch the binding in place on the wrong side on to the machine stitching, then stitch across the mitres (fig 5).

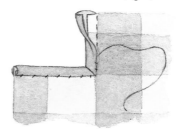

fig 5

Outside corners

1 With right sides together, stitch the binding to the edge of the fabric up to the corner. Remove the work from the sewing machine.
2 Fold the binding back on itself to allow it to bend around the corner, thereby forming a pleat in the binding. Stitch, starting again at the corner at the point

where you stopped before and continuing to the end (fig 6). Press the binding and seam towards the edge.
3 Fold the binding over the edge to the wrong side of the fabric. Turn under the cut edge of the binding and slip stitch down on to the machine stitching.
4 Form mitres at the corners and slip stitch them in place (fig 7).

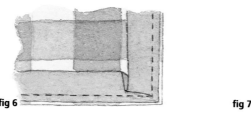

fig 6

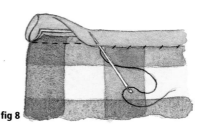

fig 7

Six-way binding

A six-way binding is a very attractive and neat way to finish off the edges of garments. As there are six thicknesses of fabric involved, the fabric chosen for the binding should be very fine and soft. This is an ideal way of finishing the neck edge of a collarless blouse or the armhole edge on a sleeveless top.

1 Cut the required length of binding strips on the true cross of the fabric. The strip should be six times the desired width of the finished binding.
2 Fold the strip in half lengthways with wrong sides together and press lightly.
3 Trim the seam allowance on the garment to slightly less than the finished width of the binding.
4 With right sides facing, line up the cut edges of the binding with the edge of the fabric; pin and tack in position.
5 Stitch along the seamline.

6 Turn the strip over the cut edge to the wrong side of the garment to form a neat folded edge. Slip stitch to the machine stitching of the seam (fig 8).

fig 8

trimmings

Trimmings can liven up some of the simplest designs and make them more exciting and interesting. Haberdashery departments are brimming with trimmings of all kinds: ribbons, laces, broderie Anglaise, fringes, tassels, tapes and many more. You can also make up several different trimmings yourself, so that they will match your sewing needs exactly.

Cords

Cords have many applications. They can be used on their own with a tassel on the end, as a pull for blinds or light switches; they make an attractive finish to the edge of cushions; and, looped on curtain headings, they add a finishing touch. There are a lot of cords on the market in various colours and thicknesses, but these are not always exactly right for a particular project. By making your own, you have a much better chance of a good match. There are several types of cord which can be made by hand.

Twisted cord

A twisted cord is the easiest type to make. The thickness and texture can be altered by using different threads.

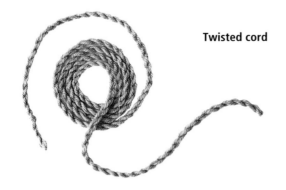

1 Cut as many strands of threads as are needed to make the desired thickness of cord, each three times the finished length you require.
2 Knot the strands together at both ends and loop one end over a hook or door knob. Stretch the cord tightly and place a pencil between the strands at the opposite end.
3 Holding the pencil close to the knots and keeping the strands taut, revolve the pencil clockwise (fig 1), until the strands are twisted tightly together along their whole length.
4 Still keep the cord taut. Grip the centre of the twisted strands and walk to meet the other end. Take hold of this end of the cord, hold the two knots in one hand and the folded end in the other (fig 2).
5 Now let the folded end go. The cord will form its own twist (fig 3). Tie the knotted ends together firmly.

revolve pencil

fig 1

fold in half

fig 2

fig 3

Finger cord

A finger cord is a hand-knotted cord consisting of a chain of loops. You slot the loops of thread into each other in turn, use your fingers instead of hooks to pull through the loops. The process requires a little thought and practice, but is then quite simple to do and very effective when finished. Two threads of the same colour may be used, or try experimenting with two different colours to form a variegated cord.

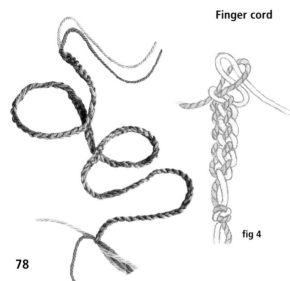

fig 4

1 Knot two pieces of thread together at one end. Take hold of the knot between the thumb and second finger of your right hand.
2 Loop the left-hand thread over your forefinger; keep hold of the end of this strand with your third and fourth fingers.
3 With your left hand, insert the forefinger into the loop and bring through the opposite strand, then hold the end of this strand with the third and fourth fingers of your left hand.
4 Now take hold of the knot with your left hand and release the loop held by your right forefinger, pulling the thread tightly to form the cord.
5 Repeat steps 2–4 until the cord is the desired length (fig 4).

Ribbon work

Ribbon work is a very simple but effective method of trimming. Because the ribbon or tape is woven, it has selveges which will not fray and can be laid on to the fabric in a single thickness. Part of its attraction is derived from the fact that it is not on the bias and therefore resists turning curves and will not lie down smoothly, as bias tape would, producing a curling-up and textured effect.

1 Mark out a design on tissue paper. The design should be very free and rather basic. Pin the tissue-paper design over the marked positions on the fabric.

2 Carefully pin the ribbon in position over the marked tissue-paper design, using the pins at right angles to the ribbon. Allow plenty of ribbon to go around the curves.

3 Tack the ribbon in position. Sew carefully down both sides of the ribbon, using either a straight stitch or small zigzag stitch.

4 Wherever the ribbon needs to be cut, turn under the cut edges and tuck in the corners to give a tidy finish, and stitch over. When all the design has been stitched, tear away the tissue paper.

A different effect is obtained when the ribbon is sewn on using only one line of stitching down the centre of the ribbon (fig 5), allowing it to curl over at the edges to give a more textured look.

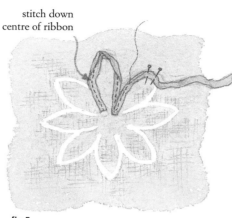

stitch down centre of ribbon

fig 5

Adding a flat trim

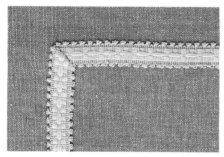

Braid, ribbon and tape can be topstitched to fabric quickly, either to decorate a cushion cover or to go around a tablecloth or napkin. Neat mitred corners are essential for a professional finish.

1 Pin and tack the trim right side up, along the first edge up to the corner. Stitch along the outer edge.

2 At the corner, fold the trim straight back over the stitched length. Working from the corner point, stitch diagonally across the trim. Cut off the excess trim

close to the stitching (fig 6).

3 Fold back the trim along the next edge. Stitch across each corner diagonally as before. Join the trim together to fit. Stitch along the inner edge of the trim (fig 7) to anchor it firmly in position.

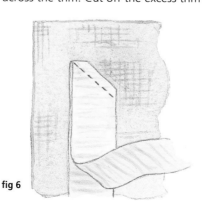

fig 6

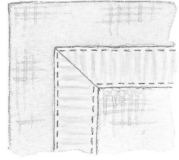

fig 7

fringing

Fringing is an attractive edging which can be made either from the threads of the main fabric or as a separate trimming. Tassels and pompons also provide a decorative, fringed trimming. All are quick to make from a variey of colourful yarns and threads.

Self fringe

This is made by removing either the weft or warp threads at the edge of a piece of fabric. Not all fabrics are suitable for this treatment: wool or linen fabrics with an even weave are the best types to use, but it is always wise to test out the process on a spare piece of fabric first. A fine wool scarf can be made quickly by this method.

1 Make sure that the edge of the fabric is cut absolutely straight.
2 Decide how long the fringe should be and make a row of machine stitches along this line to prevent the fringe growing longer than you want.

3 Using a pin, carefully remove the threads which lie parallel to this row of stitching, starting at the edge of the fabric and working inwards until you reach the stitching line. Press the fringe to remove any wrinkles.

Ready-made fringe

A ready-made fringe will often have a decorative top edge which is meant to be seen. Simply hand stitch the fringe on top of the finished edge of the fabric. You may need to work two rows of stitching. Alternatively, the fringe can be sandwiched into a seam and stitched in place when the seam is sewn. At the ends, turn in the fringe and stitch securely to prevent it unravelling.

Knotted fringe

Knotted fringes can be made using all kinds of threads and yarns. Wool, silk, cotton and rayon are all suitable, but for the best results you should match the thread to the fabric in both type and weight.

1 Cut out a cardboard strip to the depth of the intended fringe. Wrap the thread around the cardboard.
2 Use sharp scissors to cut through a few strands of the thread (fig 1).

3 Take a fine crochet hook and poke it through the fabric. Pick up a few strands of thread and fold them in half over the hook (fig 2), then pull them a little way through the fabric using the hook. With the hook still through the loop of threads, pick up the cut ends of the threads and pull them through the loop (fig 3). Pull the knot tight.
4 Continue in this way along the length of the fabric edge, using the same number of threads each time (fig 4). With thick threads, it may be easier to use one thread at a time.

A second set of knots can be made by knotting half the strands from one knot with half the strands from the adjacent knot. On a long fringe this can be repeated several times. Extra thread will be needed to allow for the extra knots, so make a test piece before calculating the length of thread required.

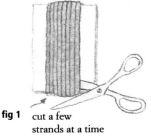

fig 1 *cut a few strands at a time*

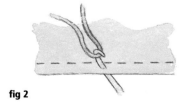

fig 2

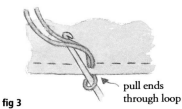

fig 3   *pull ends through loop*

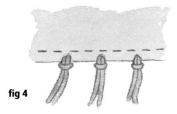

fig 4

Tassels

Tassels are a popular trimming that moves in and out of fashion. They can be used in a variety of decorative ways. Individually, they may be used as pullers for blinds or zips, or on the corners of cushions. Joined in a row, they can make an attractive fringe.

1 Wind a length of thread around a piece of card to the depth of the required tassel. If making more than one tassel, count the number of 'winds' so that all the tassels will be the same size.
2 Thread a tapestry needle with a very long thread and work a line of backstitch a short way down from the top of the wound threads.

3 Hold the top of the card tightly and cut the threads along base edge (fig 5). Remove the card and you will have a little skirt of threads.
4 If joining to a cord, wrap the skirt around the knot in your cord. This can be padded to make a larger head.
5 Stitch through the top of the skirt and the knot several times. Wrap a thread around the tassel several times, about one-third of the way below the knot.
6 Thread a blunt needle with either matching or contrasting thread and work a row of blanket stitch loosely around the 'head' of the tassel. Now work a second row of blanket stitches into the loops of the first row.
7 Continue working blanket stitch around the head (fig 6), loosening and tightening the stitches as necessary to keep the rounded shape. Fasten off when the tassel head has been covered.

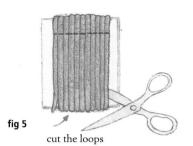

fig 5

cut the loops

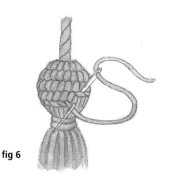

fig 6

Pompons

Pompons are purely decorative and are great fun. Like tassels, they can be used as pullers at the bottom of a blind or for a light switch. They can be made from most knitting or embroidery yarns. Children love making pompons, and they provide an enjoyable occupation for rainy days.

If making several pompons which need to be the same size, you should count the number of 'winds' around the rings and repeat this number. You must also keep the tension of the wool the same, as a looser tension makes a bigger pompon.

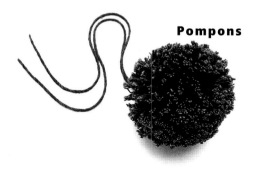

1 Cut out two circles of strong card to the required size. Cut out a smaller circle from the centre of each one, about one-quarter the size of the original circle.

2 Put the card rings one on top of the other and wind the wool around them, threading it through the central hole (fig 7). Continue until the hole is filled.
3 Insert one blade of a sharp pair of scissors between the card rings and cut through the threads around the outside edge (fig 8).
4 Take another length of wool and place it around the strands between the card rings. Tie it very tightly and knot, leaving the ends long enough for attaching the pompon.
5 Remove the card rings and shake the pompon. Trim off any untidy ends.

wind evenly over
both rings

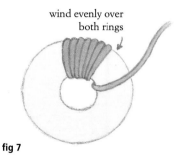

fig 7

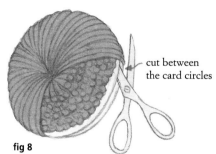

cut between
the card circles

fig 8

81

summer scarves

Scarves do not have to be limited to winter. They can be used as a fashion statement in the summer too, using fine, light fabrics in soft colours. The first scarf, with its useful pockets, is functional as well as pretty, and uses an interesting combination of linen and silk chiffon, while the self fringe makes a pleasing finishing touch. Our long, sheer scarf is made in two colours of silk chiffon.

Pocketed scarf

You will need

70cm (28in) linen fabric, 150cm (60in) wide
60cm (24in) chiffon, 150cm (60in) wide
Matching sewing threads

To cut out

1 Cut out 2 pieces of linen and 2 pieces of chiffon, each 30 x 115cm (12 x 45in).
2 Cut out 2 strips of linen, each 30 x 4cm (12 x 1½in).

To make up

1 With right sides together, join the 2 pieces of linen along the short edges. Join the 2 pieces of chiffon in the same way. Press both seams.
2 On each of the linen strips, make a row of small zigzag stitches 2.5cm (1in) in

from the long edge. Fringe below the line of stitching.
3 With right sides together, place a strip of fringing along one short end of the joined linen and stitch in place 1.5cm (⅝in) from the edge (fig 1). Repeat at the other end.
4 With right sides together, place the joined chiffon on top of the linen. Pin, tack and stitch in place with a 1.5cm (⅝in) seam allowance, leaving a very small gap for turning. Trim the seam allowance, neaten and press.
5 Turn the scarf right side out and slip stitch the gap closed. Press. Turn down 2.5cm (1in) on each of the short sides and press.
6 Fold the short ends on to the linen side by 20cm (8in) to form a pocket. Hand stitch in place along the sides (fig 2).

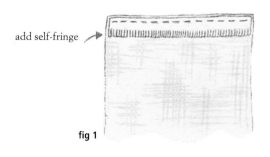

add self-fringe →

fig 1

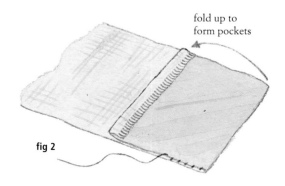

fold up to form pockets

fig 2

Sheer scarf

You will need

45cm (18in) silk chiffon, 150cm (60in) wide
45cm (18in) contrasting silk chiffon, 150cm (60in) wide
Matching sewing threads

To make up

1 With right sides together, pin and tack the 2 contrasting pieces of silk chiffon

one on top of the other.
2 Stitch around all 4 sides, leaving a very small opening on one short side, for turning. Trim the seams and neaten if necessary. Press.
3 Turn the scarf right side out. Turn in the opening and slip stitch closed.

Alternatively, cut a single length of fabric and finish with a hand-rolled hem.

winter scarves

Scarves need not always be long and flowing. These two neat little scarves, suitable for both men and women, use very small amounts of fabric and are both cosy and smart. The necktie combines panne and crushed velvet while our collar scarf is made in wool velour.

Necktie

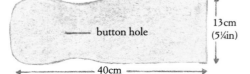

button hole

13cm
(5¼in)

40cm
(16in)

You will need
50cm (¾yd) panne velvet, 115cm (45in) wide
50cm (¾yd) crushed velvet, 115cm (45in) wide
Matching sewing threads

To scale up the pattern
Draw up the pattern using the measurements shown on the shape left.

To cut out
From panne velvet
2 shapes
From crushed velvet
2 shapes

To make up
1 With right sides together, pin, tack and stitch the short end of one panne piece to the short end of one crushed velvet piece, and press the seam open.
2 Pin and tack the same seam on the other 2 pieces of fabric. Stitch, leaving a 5cm (2in) gap in the middle for turning (fig 1, right). Press the seam open.
3 With right sides facing, place the 2 pieces together, with different fabrics facing. Pin, tack and stitch all around (fig 2, right) and trim the seam.
4 Turn to the right side through the gap in the short seam. Roll the edges between finger and thumb to make sure that the seam comes right to the edge, and press. Ladder stitch the gap closed.

To finish
Make a buttonhole 5cm (2in) long centrally in the necktie, 6cm (2½in) in from one end (fig 3, right).

Collar scarf

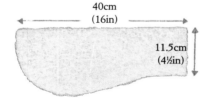

40cm
(16in)

11.5cm
(4½in)

You will need
40 x 30cm (16 x 12in) wool velour
40 x 30cm (16 x 12in) silk, for lining
Matching sewing threads
1 button

To scale up the pattern
Draw up the pattern using the measurements shown on the shape left.

To cut out
From main fabric
2 shapes
From lining
2 shapes
1 strip 10 x 2cm (4 x ¾in) on the cross

To make up
1 Make up the rouleau from the strip of lining and turn to the right side. Pin and tack the rouleau to the fabric 6cm (2½in) along one long straight edge.
2 Join one short end of a main fabric piece to the short end of the other main fabric piece. Trim 3cm (1¼in) off the straight edge of the lining and then join the corresponding seams.
3 With right sides together, pin, tack and machine stitch the lining to the main fabric along the long straight edge, catching in the rouleau.
4 Match the cut edges of the curved side of the lining to the cut edges of the curved side of the main fabric; there will be a small margin of fabric on the wrong side. Pin, tack and machine stitch around the seam, leaving a small gap for turning. Trim the seam.
5 Turn to the right side and pull the curved seam over to the edge. This will bring the top fabric round to the back along the straight edge. Slipstitch the gap. Press.

To finish
Sew a button to the left-hand side to correspond with the loop, making sure the bottom edges of the scarf line up.

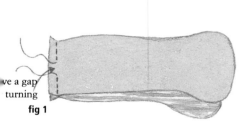

ve a gap
turning

fig 1

fig 2

fig 3

pelmet

This jolly pelmet with its trimming of pompons would brighten up any room, particularly one for a child. Choose a brightly coloured fabric with a pattern that lends itself to this design. Measure the length of the pelmet and divide by the chosen size of the triangular points, so that they will fit exactly across the length. The pelmet shown is approximately 55cm (22in) deep.

You will need

Fabric to desired width of pelmet plus twice the seam allowance x desired depth plus 11.5cm (4½in) for turnings. 2 widths of fabric may be required
Matching sewing thread
Lining fabric to same measurements as main fabric
Card for template
Yarn in a variety of colours, for pompons

To cut out and prepare the fabric

Straighten up the main fabric and the lining. Cut out the fabric and lining to the required length. Join the widths with plain, flat seams if necessary, pressing the seams open.

To make up

1 Place the lining on the table right side up and lay the main fabric over it, wrong side up and with the cut edges matching.
2 Decide on size you want the points to be and make a template of one point in card. Try to make the points fit in with the fabric design if possible; you may need to adjust the width of the pelmet at this stage so that the points fit across it exactly.
3 On the wrong side of the fabric, work across the width of the pelmet, drawing around the template for all the points. Tack together the main fabric and lining close to this line. Stitch along the line and up the side edges of the pelmet.
4 Cut away the fabric below the points, leaving 6mm (¼in) for turning (fig 1). Clip into the angles. Turn the pelmet to the right side and press.
5 Tack along the top edge through the lining and main fabric to hold them together. Turn over 10cm (4in) and tack along the fold line. Turn under the cut edge by 1.5cm (⅝in), then pin, tack and stitch along this line (fig 2).

To finish

1 Make pompons following the instructions on page 81 and stitch to the points of the pelmet, alternating the different colours (fig 3).
2 Hang threaded on a pole or attached with clips on curtain rings.

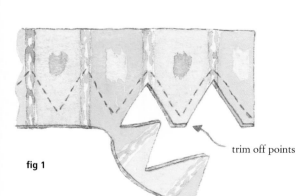

trim off points

fig 1

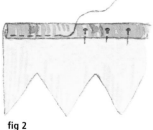

fig 2

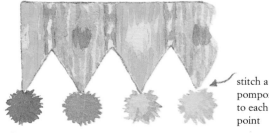

stitch a pompon to each point

fig 3

jacket

A loose-fitting jacket with a generous bound edge is a useful addition to any wardrobe, as it can be casual or dressed up for more formal occasions. By choosing different fabrics, the same pattern can be made up for day or evening wear.

You will need

2.7m (3yd) fabric, 115cm (45in) wide
Matching sewing thread
1.2m (1⅓yd) interfacing, 90cm (36in) wide
Bias binding (optional)

To scale up the pattern

Draw up the patterns using the measurements shown on the shapes below. Alternatively, turn to page 104 and scale up the patterns from the diagrams.

To cut out

From fabric
1 pair fronts
1 back
2 sleeves
2 pockets
2 front bands
2 front band facings
From interfacing
2 front bands

To make and attach the pockets

1 Neaten the top edge of each pocket piece by overlocking or turning under the cut edge and stitching.

2 Turn over 2.5cm (1in) at the top of the pocket to the right side. Stitch down the sides of this fold on the seamline (fig 1). Trim and press.

3 Turn the pocket to the wrong side and turn in the seam allowance on the 3 cut edges, mitring the corners. Tack.

4 Place each pocket on a jacket front piece, 6cm (2½in) in from the side edge and 9cm (3½in) up from the bottom edge. Pin, tack and stitch the pocket into position.

It may help to interface the top fold of the pocket to give it a little more body. You could also stitch the fold down so that it is visible from the right side, and slip stitch the pockets on to the front of the jacket if you do not like to see the machine stitching that holds the pockets in place on the right side.

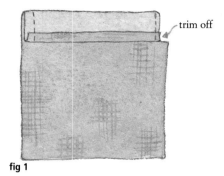

trim off

fig 1

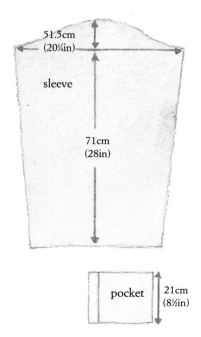

51.5cm (20¼in)

sleeve

71cm (28in)

pocket   21cm (8½in)

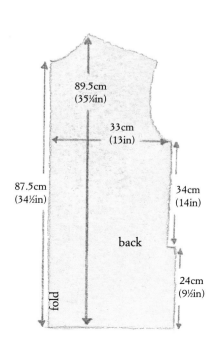

89.5cm (35¼in)

33cm (13in)

87.5cm (34½in)

34cm (14in)

back

24cm (9½in)

fold

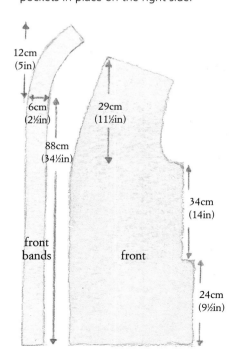

12cm (5in)

6cm (2½in)

88cm (34½in)

29cm (11½in)

front bands

34cm (14in)

front

24cm (9½in)

To attach the front band

1 Pin, tack and stitch the shoulder seams of the jacket (fig 2).

2 With right sides together, pin the interfacing to the front bands. Join the front bands at centre back (fig 3). Join the front band facings at centre back.

3 Pin, tack and stitch the facing to the front band.

4 With right sides together, pin, tack and stitch the front band to the jacket, along the front and around the neck edge. Turn the facing to the wrong side and slip stitch in place on to the machine stitching, leaving the bottom few centimetres (inches) free (fig 4).

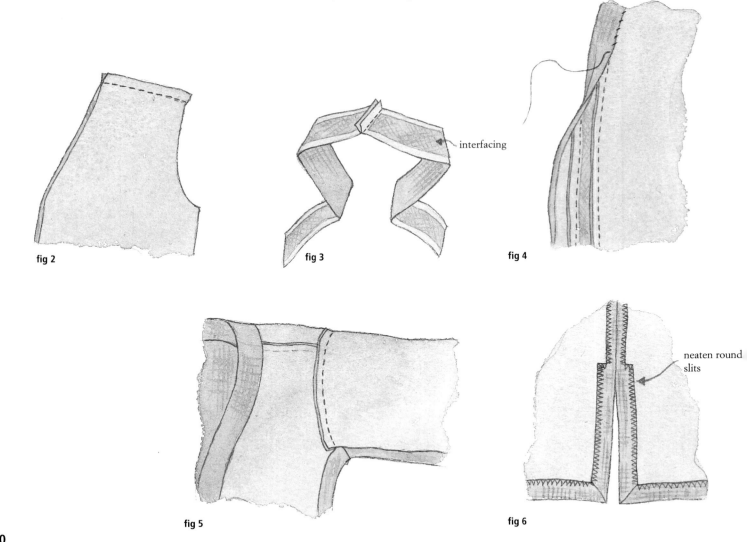

fig 2

interfacing

fig 3

fig 4

fig 5

neaten round slits

fig 6

To set in the sleeves

1 With right sides together, pin, tack and stitch each sleeve to the jacket, matching the centre point at the top of the sleeve with the shoulder seam (fig 5, left). Neaten the seam by overlocking or with bias binding.

2 Join each side seam of the jacket and the sleeve seam in one stage, leaving open a 23cm (9in) slit at the bottom edge of the jacket. Press the seam open and neaten with overlocking or zigzag stitching. Neaten the slits at the same time (fig 6) as neatening the side seams.

3 Turn under 12cm (5in) at the bottom edge of each sleeve and machine or slip stitch in place. Fold up to make cuffs.

To finish

Open out the front band. Trim hem allowance on the band facings. Turn up a 2.5cm (1in) hem and slipstitch in place. Slipstitch slit facings. Slipstitch the bottom of the front bands.

cushions

The easiest cushions to make are those that can be stitched together quickly without the addition of complicated fastenings. To achieve this with style and panache, different fabrics and trimmings can be cut and fitted together with clever seaming, or quickly applied using a few sewing-machine skills. Add a selection of unusual and imaginative fastenings and you have the perfect cushion cover.

Triangular cushion

In this unusual cushion, two opposing triangular sections fold over the cushion front and fasten together at the front to hold the cushion pad in place. Mix and match plain and striped fabrics for an up-to-the-minute look.

back — 52cm (20½in) · 52cm (20½in) · 30cm (12in)

front — 53.5cm (21in) · 52cm (20½in) · 31.5cm (12⅜in)

flap

You will need
60cm (24in) plain cotton furnishing fabric, 150cm (60in) wide
55cm (22in) square striped cotton furnishing fabric
Matching sewing threads
50cm (20in) square cushion pad
Button or other decorative fastening

To scale up the pattern
Draw up the patterns using the measurements shown on the shapes left.

To cut out
From plain fabric
1 back
2 flaps
From striped fabric
1 front

To make up
1 Place one flap piece to one side of the front piece; pin and tack together (fig 1). Stitch in from each side for 5cm (2in) only and press the seam open. Turn under a 6mm (¼in) double hem on the front piece and stitch in place.
2 With right sides facing, place the remaining flap piece to the opposite side of the front piece and join together. Press the seam open.
3 With right sides together, position the back piece over the front piece with flaps. Pin, tack and stitch all round the outer edge, taking a 1.5cm (⅝in) seam allowance (fig 2). Trim seam allowance and turn the cover right side out.
4 Pin, tack and topstitch across the cover, along the flap edge on the

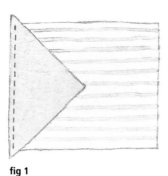

fig 1

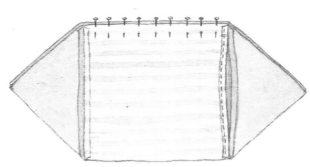

fig 2

opening side of the front piece and along the front piece on the opposite side. Stitch close to the seamlines on both sides.
5 Insert the cushion pad into the cover and fasten the two flaps over the front with a button.

Four-cornered cushion

Clever seaming matches the stripes of this cushion together following the shape of the flap, so that they meet together at the centre when the cover is fastened.

You will need
60cm (24in) plain cotton furnishing
    fabric, 150cm (60in) wide
60cm (24in) striped cotton furnishing
    fabric, 150cm (60in) wide
Matching sewing threads
50cm (20in) square cushion pad
Button or other decorative fastening

To scale up the pattern
Draw up the patterns using the measurements shown on page 92.

To cut out
From plain fabric
1 front and 4 flaps
1 facing 52 x 16cm (20½ x 6¼in)
From striped fabric
1 back
8 half flaps – allow for centre joins

To make up
1 Join the half flap pieces together in pairs, matching the pattern across the central seamline. Press the seams open.
2 With right sides facing, stitch the striped flaps to the plain flaps, taking a 1.5cm (⅝in) seam allowance and leaving the base edge open. Trim the seam allowance and turn right side out. Press.
3 Stitch a 6mm (¼in) double hem along one long edge of the facing. Repeat along one side edge of the front piece.
4 Lay out the back right side up. Pin and tack the flaps, striped side down, on each side of the back piece. Place the front piece right side down over the flaps, matching cut edges to cut edges and the hemmed edge against the seamline on one side.
5 Place the facing right side down over the hemmed edge of the front, with the cut edge matching the cut edge of the back. Stitch all round. Turn the cover right side out and tuck the flap inside.
6 Insert the cushion pad, fold the flaps to meet in the centre and fasten with a decorative button.

Rouleau cushion

Although the front of this cushion looks as though it fastens with tiny buttons, this is just an illusion. There is a back opening similar to the Ribbon-work cushion on page 96.

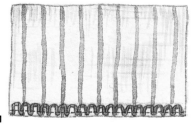

fig 1

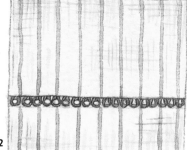

fig 2

You will need
60cm (24in) striped cotton furnishing
    fabric, 150cm (60in) wide
1.2m (1⅜yd) navy tape, 1cm (⅜in)
    wide
Matching sewing thread
50cm (20in) square cushion pad
18 buttons

To cut out
From striped fabric, cut out 2 backs, each 53 x 28.5cm (21¼ x 11¼in), 1 front 53 x 36cm (21¼ x 14¾in) and 1 front 53 x 20cm (21¼ x 8in).

To make up
1 Tack a row of stitches along the seamline, 1.5cm (⅝in) from one long edge of the larger front piece. Fold the tape exactly in half lengthways and pin and stitch the edges together. Form the tape into 18 3cm (1¼in) loops along the long tacked edge of the front piece, with the loops facing inwards. Check that the loops are evenly spaced and equal in size. Pin and tack in position (fig 1).
2 With right sides facing, lay the smaller front piece over the looped front piece. Pin, tack and stitch the fronts together along the looped edge, catching the loops firmly in place. Trim and press the seam open, with the loops over the smaller front piece (fig 2).
3 Make up the back piece following steps 5 and 6 for the Ribbon work Cushion on page 96. Hand sew a button inside each loop on the front, to give the impression that it is fastened by the loop.

Ribbon work cushion

At the back of this cushion, one side folds neatly over the other to form an envelope-type opening, so the cushion pad can be slotted inside the cover quickly and easily. The decorative tape is stitched haphazardly in flower shapes inside a border, creating an unstructured but effective design.

You will need
Tissue paper
60cm (24in) plain cotton furnishing fabric, 150cm (60in) wide
Approximately 10.6m (11¾yd) plain tape, 1.5cm (½in) wide
Matching sewing thread
50cm (20in) square cushion pad

To scale up the pattern
Draw up the flower motif shape on page 97 and trace it off 8 times on to tissue paper.

To cut out
From plain fabric, cut out 2 backs, each 53 x 28.5cm (21¼ x 11¼in), and 1 front 53cm (21¼in) square.

To make up
1 Lightly mark a straight line 6cm (2½in) in from the outer edges all around the front piece. Beginning at one corner, position the plain tape centrally over this line, then pin and stitch in place down the centre of the tape. At each corner, fold the tape into a loop and stitch down. At the last corner, trim off the tape. Tuck under the cut end and stitch in place.
2 Position the 8 tissue-paper flower motifs inside the outline tape on the front piece and move them about until they are arranged to your satisfaction. Pin and then tack the motifs in place, tacking diagonally across the centre of each piece.
3 Cut approximately 1m (1yd) of tape for each flower. Lay the tape over the marked outline and stitch in place down the centre of the tape. Curve the tape carefully around the petal shapes as you stitch, varying their size and shape so that each individual flower will look slightly different.
4 When each flower has been stitched, gently tear away the tissue paper. Cut approximately 15cm (6in) of tape for each flower centre. Stitch in place down the centre of the tape, curling the tape around to form a tight circle. Fasten off, tucking under the cut end.
5 Turn under a 6mm (¼in) double hem on one long edge of each back piece and stitch in place. With right sides up, overlap the hemmed edges of the back pieces for 8cm (3¼in). Pin and tack together.
6 Place the front and back together with right sides facing. Pin, tack and stitch together all around the outer edge, taking a 1.5cm (⅝in) seam allowance. Trim the edges. Undo the tacking down the centre back and turn the cover right side out. Press. Insert the cushion pad through the back opening.

Pattern diagrams

On the following pages you will find pattern diagrams and cutting layouts for those designs where more than just a simple cutting outline is required. These diagrams complement the instructions given for the wrap-around skirt, drawstring trousers, shirts and jacket.

Flower motif for ribbon work cushion

wrap-around skirt

The dimensions on page 46 and the pattern pieces in the pattern diagram (right) are for a size 10. As the skirt wraps over at the front this size will also fit a size 12. To make a larger size add 1.3cm (½in) to each of the side seams. To make a smaller size reduce each seam by the same amount.

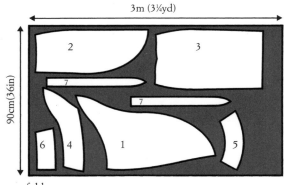

3m (3¼yd)

90cm (36in)

2

3

7

7

6 4 1 5

fold

cutting layout

1 right front
2 left front
3 back
4 right front facing
5 left front facing
6 back facing
7 ties

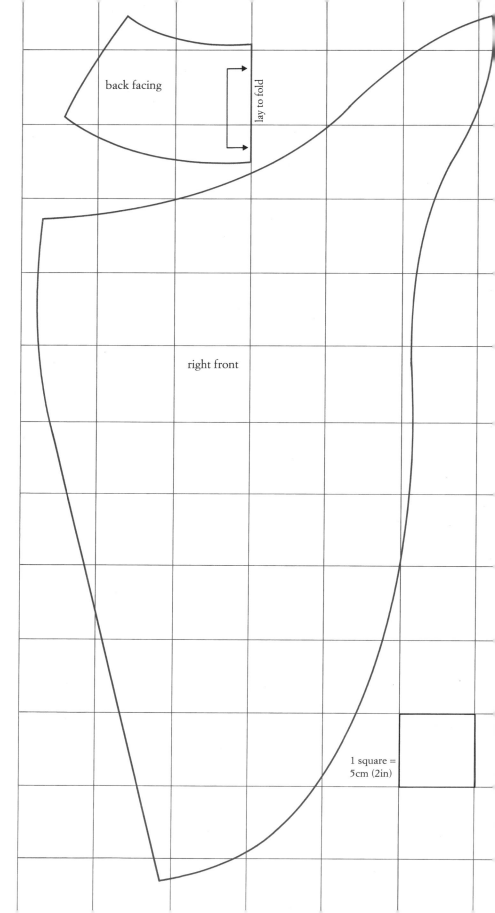

back facing

lay to fold

right front

1 square = 5cm (2in)

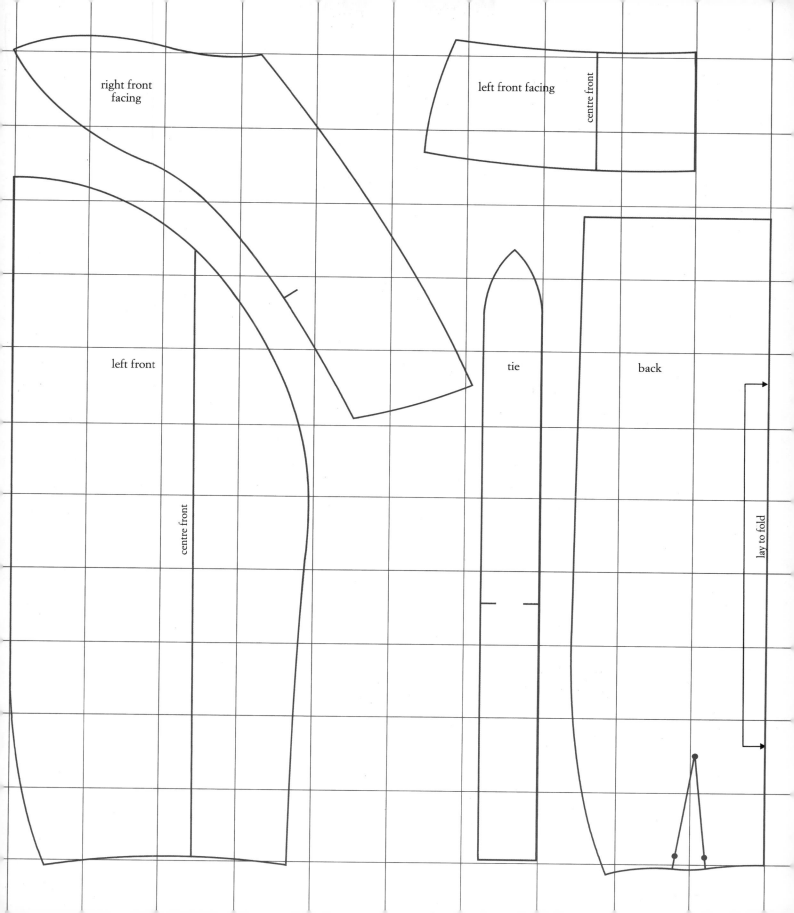

right front facing

left front facing

centre front

left front

centre front

tie

back

lay to fold

drawstring trousers

The dimensions on page 54 and the pattern pieces on the pattern diagram (right) are for a size 12-14, but because of their loose fitting shape these trousers should fit most people. Before cutting out the pattern pieces, however, check the leg length as these may need adjusting.

1 square = 5cm (2in)

waistband

eyelets

pocket

straight grain

2.5m (3yd)

115 cm(45in)

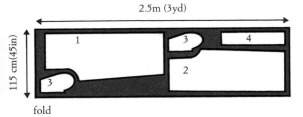

fold

cutting layout

1 front
2 back
3 pocket
4 waistband

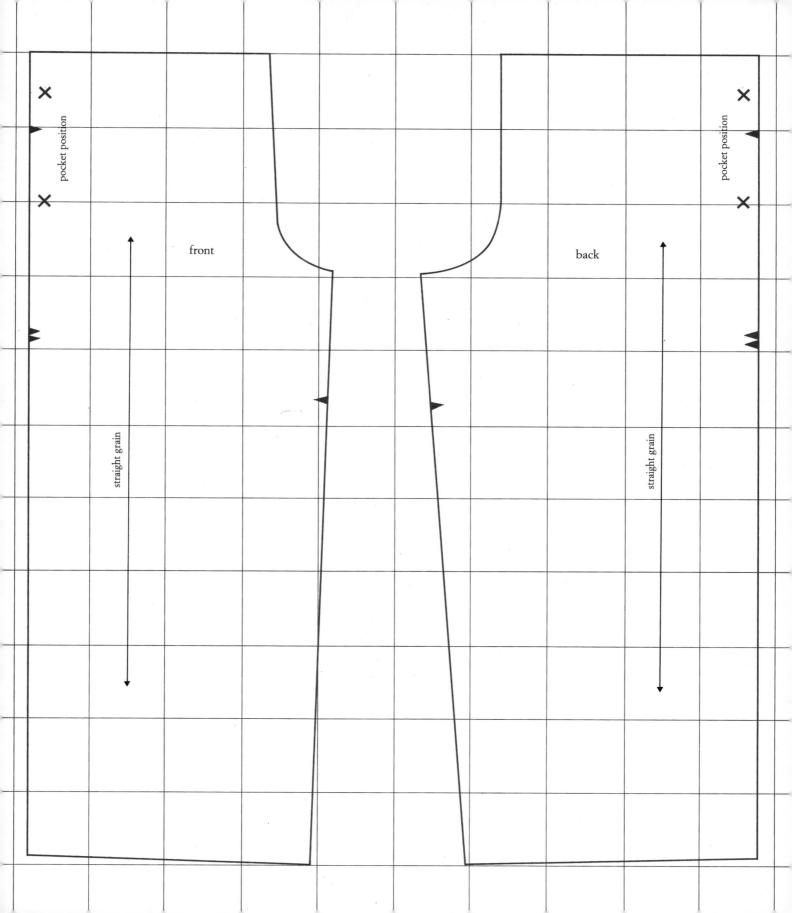

pocket position

front

back

pocket position

straight grain

straight grain

shirts

The dimensions on pages 63 and 65 and the pattern pieces on the pattern diagram (right) are for sizes 12-16. Before cutting out the pattern pieces check the bust measurement and sleeve length and adjust if necessary. To make a larger size, add 1.3cm (½in) to each seam or to the overall sleeve length. For a smaller size, reduce by the same amount.

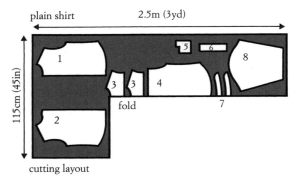

plain shirt   2.5m (3yd)

115cm (45in)

fold

cutting layout

1 left front
2 right front
3 yoke
4 back
5 placket
6 cuff
7 collar
8 sleeve

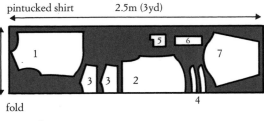

pintucked shirt   2.5m (3yd)

115cm (45in)

fold

cutting layout

1 front
2 back
3 yoke
4 collar
5 placket
6 cuff
7 sleeve

102

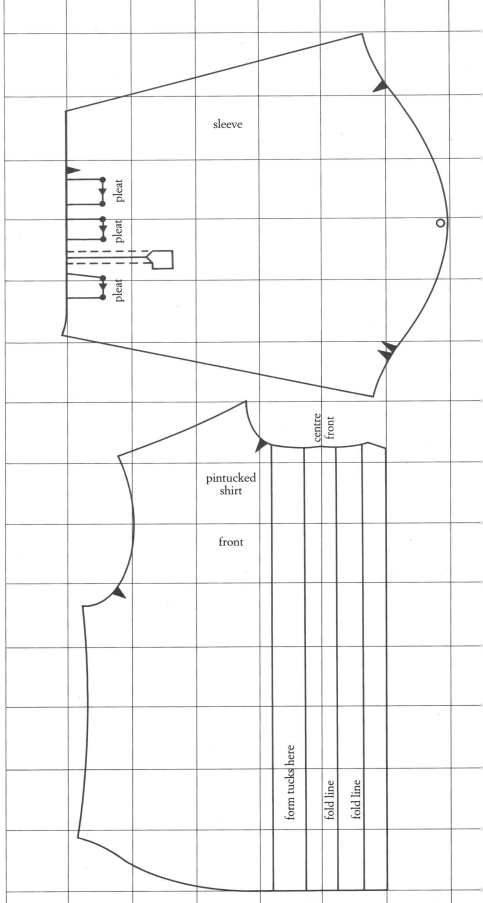

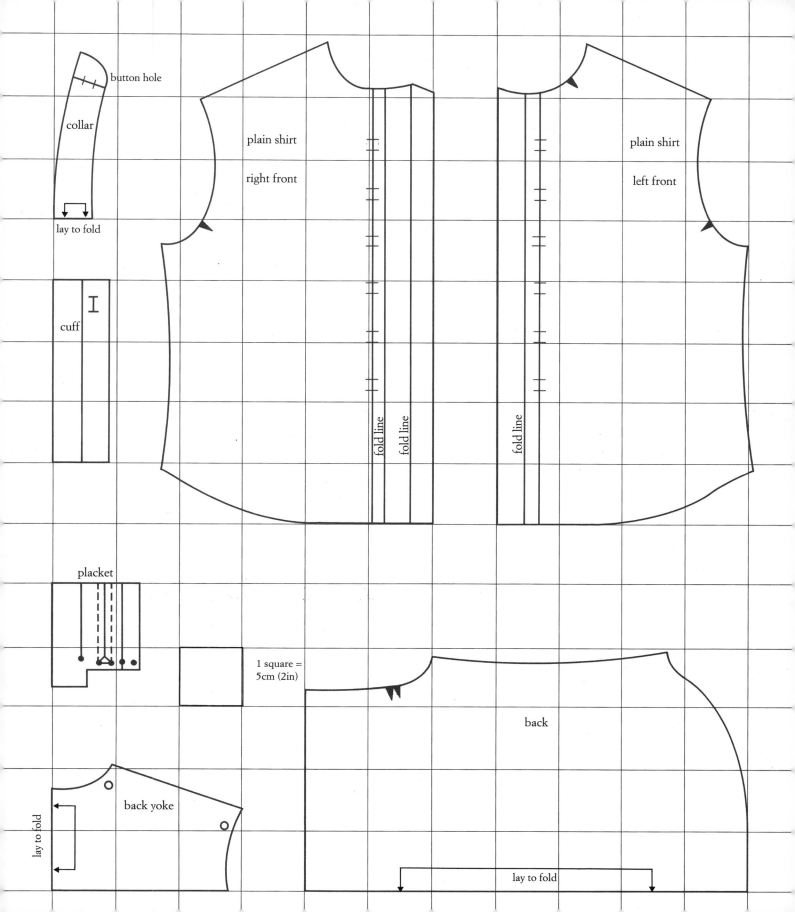

button hole

collar

lay to fold

cuff

plain shirt

right front

fold line fold line

plain shirt

left front

fold line

placket

1 square =
5cm (2in)

back

back yoke

lay to fold

lay to fold

jacket

The dimensions on page 88 and the pattern pieces on the pattern diagram (right) are for size 12-14. To make a larger size add 1.3cm (½in) to each of the side seams. To make a smaller size reduce each seam by the same amount.

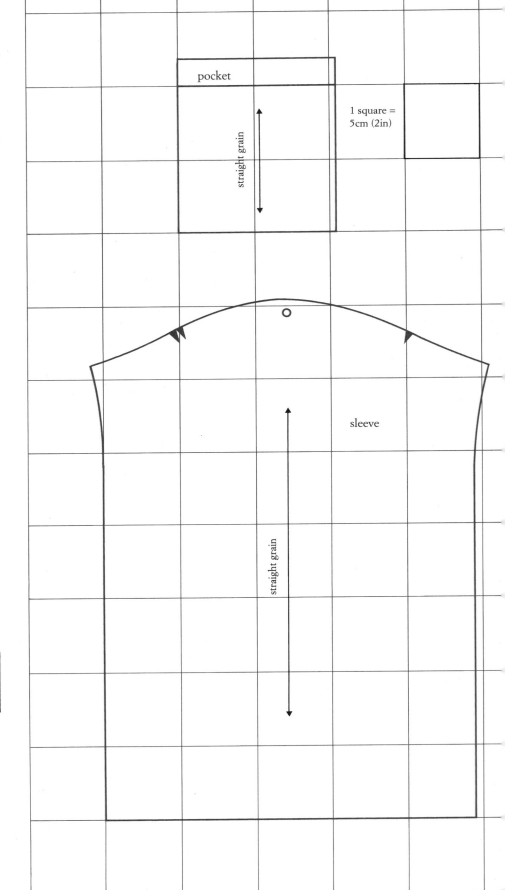

pocket

1 square = 5cm (2in)

straight grain

sleeve

straight grain

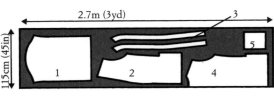

2.7m (3yd)

3

5

115cm (45in)

1   2   4

fold

cutting layout

1 sleeve
2 front
3 front bands
4 back
104   5 pocket

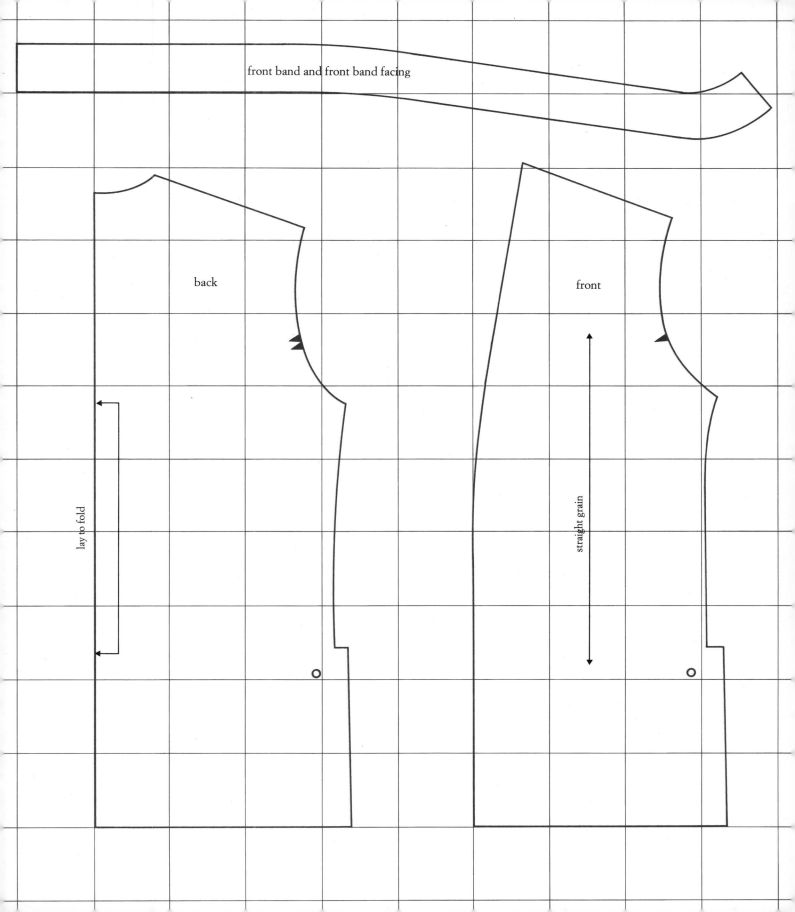

front band and front band facing

back

front

lay to fold

straight grain

glossary of fabrics

Acetate Made from cellulose. It is often used to make linings.

Acrilan A trade name for acrylic fibres.

Acrylic The generic name for fibres made from the liquid chemical acrylonitrile, which resemble wool and are often used for knitted garments. Acrylic fibres can also be woven.

Alpaca The very fine, soft hair of the alpaca – a type of llama – is very expensive and is woven into a luxurious fabric, used for expensive coats and jackets. Because of the high cost, it is usually mixed with sheep's wool for economy.

Angora The soft, fluffy hair of the Angora rabbit is often used for knitted garments such as jumpers and cardigans.

Astrakhan Originally the name applied to the fleece of lambs from Astrakhan, this curly wool is usually black or brown in colour and was used to make coats and hats. Nowadays, the term usually denotes a fabric which imitates this fleece and is used to make hats, coats and collars.

Barathea A closely woven, medium-weight fabric made from the finest wool and available in plain colours only. It has a smooth, almost shiny appearance and is used to make suits, skirts and lightweight coats.

Batiste A very fine, sheer fabric made from the finest linen or cotton and used to make handkerchiefs, lingerie, night wear, blouses and fine baby clothes.

Bouclé A looped yarn which may be woven or knitted into a fabric with a raised, loopy finish that is both attractive and very warm. The yarn can be made from wool or synthetic fibres, or a mixture of the two, and is used to make coats, dresses and suits.

Brocade Originally made from silk, and now from synthetics as well, this fairly stiff fabric is produced on a Jacquard loom. The satin weave appears alternately on the front and back of the fabric to create the design, often depicting flowers or leaves; metallic threads are sometimes woven into the pattern. Brocade is used for evening wear and the heavier types for furnishings.

Broderie Anglaise Traditionally made in white cotton, with white embroidered eyelets forming the pattern, broderie Anglaise can now also be made from synthetic fabrics or mixtures. The white embroidery is sometimes replaced by pastel colours. It is used to make baby clothes, children's dresses and blouses, and is also available as a trimming in narrow widths for use as an edging or insertion, combined with narrow ribbon.

Brushed cotton This fabric is produced in exactly the way that its name suggests, with the brushing lifting the fibres to produce a warm, soft fabric that is used to make night wear and blouses.

Buckram A stiffened fabric which in turn is used to stiffen other fabrics in belts, hats and curtain headings. It is available in various weights, the coarsest being made from hessian and the lightest from cotton.

Butter muslin A very cheap, loosely woven cotton fabric, originally used for straining milk for butter. Muslin makes light and floaty bed curtains.

Calico A cheap, strong, woven cotton first produced in Calicut, India. It is usually sold unbleached and undyed, when it is easily recognized by its oatmeal-like appearance. Today, dyed versions are also available. Calico is often used in home furnishings or to make dressmaking toiles.

Cambric A fine, closely woven fabric made from linen or, more usually, cotton. It has a slightly glazed surface on one side and is usually available in plain colours. It is used to make baby clothes, night wear and blouses.

Camel Originally the name for a very expensive and luxurious fabric made from camel hair, and often mixed with wool for economy. It is very soft but also very light and warm, and is used mainly to make coats. The term is now also applied to thick, camel-coloured woollen fabrics.

Candlewick A shaggy, loose-piled fabric produced by pulling tufts through a loosely woven base fabric. Generally made from cotton, it may now also be synthetic, and is used to make bedspreads and dressing gowns.

Cashmere The hair of the Cashmere goat is woven into this most beautiful soft, fine fabric, recognized by its smooth, silky finish. As a yarn, it is knitted into luxurious jerseys and cardigans. The fabric is very light yet also very warm, and is used mainly to make men's and ladies' suits and coats. Extremely expensive, it is often mixed with sheep's wool for economy.

Cavalry twill A very strong wollen fabric with a twill weave, now sometimes made from acrylics. It was originally used to make riding breeches and is still in demand for hardwearing trousers.

Challis Made from fine wool, this lovely fabric is light in weight and suitable for making dresses and shawls. It is available in plain colours or printed.

Chambray A soft cotton fabric with a coloured warp thread and white weft. It is similar to denim, but much lighter in weight and not as strong, and is very often pale blue in colour. Chambray is used to make shirts, dresses and children's clothes.

Chamois A very soft leather cloth, usually tan in colour, made from the skin of a small mountain goat. fabric is sometimes woven to imitate it and is given the same name.

Cheesecloth A loosely woven, rather rough cotton cloth which was originally used to wrap cheeses. As a fashion fabric, it is more closely woven and can be dyed. It is used to make flimsy trousers and dresses and is very cheap.

Chenille With a hairy pile all round, this yarn derives its name from the French word for 'caterpillar'. It can be made from a variety of fibres including silk, cotton, wool, viscose and various mixtures. The yarn is often used for knitting; when woven, it has a thick, velvety pile and is usually used for soft furnishings, but also occasionally as a fashion fabric.

Chiffon A very soft, very fine fabric originally made from silk but now also from synthetic fibres. It is available in a wide range of usually plain colours, sometimes with graduated shading known as 'ombre'. Chiffon drapes beautifully and is used for making scarves and soft, floaty garments.

Chino A firm, closely woven cotton fabric with a twill weave, originally used for summer uniforms for the armed forces. Often still available in army khaki and beige, it is very hardwearing and is used for making trousers and casual wear.

Chintz Traditionally a cotton fabric printed with a large design of flowers or birds and sometimes glazed with a special finish, chintz is used to make curtains and loose covers. Nowadays the term is also applied to glazed cotton fabrics in plain colours, and these too are used mainly for soft furnishings, especially scatter cushion covers.

Ciré The name derives from the French word for 'waxed', and the original fabric was indeed waxed to give it a shiny finish. Now the term is used for fabric which has been treated to provide a shiny finish. These fabrics are often showerproof and have a smooth, slippery feel.

Cloqué Cloque is the French wiord for 'blistered',which exactly describes the appearance of this fabric. Originally made from silk, it is now also produced from synthetics. Cloqué is used to make dresses.

Corduroy A cotton fabric recognized by the velvet ribs running along its length. These vary in thickness, fabric with the widest ribs being

known as 'jumbo cord' and the finest 'baby cord'; 'needlecord' is slightly heavier than baby cord. These are strong, hardwearing fabrics and are useful for making children's clothes, as well as skirts and trousers for adults. Although corduroys are most often produced in plain colours, needlecord is sometimes printed with attractive designs.

Cotton Produced from the seed pod of the cotton plant, cotton is processed into many different fabrics which vary greatly in quality and cost.

Cotton jersey A knitted cotton fabric, originally used mainly to make teeshirts, vests and underwear, but now also used for skirts and dresses. Thicker types are used to make sportswear.

Crêpe de Chine A luxurious fabric, originally made from silk but now also from synthetics. It is woven using a twisted yarn, which produces the characteristic crêpy feel. Available in plain colours or in beautiful prints, it can be used to make blouses, dresses and beautiful lingerie.

Cupra The name is short for cuprammonium rayon, a soft, silky fabric which is very good for lining. It is sometimes sold as Bemberg silk or Bremsilk.

Denim Taking its name from Nîmes in France, where it was first made, this very strong fabric has become universally popular for jeans,jackets and shirts. Traditionally made with a coloured – usually blue – warp thread and a white weft, it is often dyed, disguising this effect.

Devoré velvet This fabric has been chemically treated to remove, or 'devour', some of the surface of the velvet, leaving a pattern in the remaining pile. As some of the velvet has been removed, the resulting fabric is light and drapes beautifully. It is used for scarves and evening wear.

Donegal A tweed originating from County Donegal, Ireland. Made from wool, it has a speckled effect, the specks being surprisingly bright in colour; used for suits and jackets.

Drill A very strong twill-weave fabric, originally made from cotton but now often with synthetics added. It is usually made into overalls and other working garments.

Dupion A silk fabric with a slubbed effect in its surface. Often wrongly referred to as 'wild' or 'raw' silk, it is very popular for making wedding dresses, bridesmaid's outfits and ballgowns. It is surprisingly inexpensive and is available in a huge range of colours.

Egyptian cotton A very fine-quality cotton which is exceptionally smooth to the touch. It is used to make good-quality bedlinen, night wear and baby clothes.

Foullard A soft, printed twill-weave fabric, originally made from silk but now also from synthetics. It was used mainly for making ties and cravats and the prints reflect this, although the fabric is now also used for dresses and blouses.

Gaberdine A very closely woven, strong and slightly stiff twill-weave fabric which can be made from wool, cotton or synthetics. In the past school raincoats were made from wool gaberdine, the close weave making them showerproof.

Georgette A very fine, filmy fabric, similar to chiffon but woven with a twisted yarn to give it a slightly crêpy feel. It is usually made from silk and is used for garments and scarves.

Gingham A checked fabric, in which the checks have been formed by the weave. It is usually made in white with one other colour, resulting in checks in three tones. Strong and hardwearing, gingham is usually made from cotton but sometimes from synthetics. It is relatively cheap and has an attractive fresh appearance, giving it many uses, but it moves in and out of fashion.

Habutai A fine, soft, relatively cheap silk used for lining and also for making shirts.

Harris tweed
A rather rough tweed woven by hand in the crofts of the outer Hebrides, a group of islands off the coast of Scotland, of which the Isle of Harris is one. As it is made on hand looms, the fabric is only 69cm (27in) wide. It is very hardwearing, lasting for many years, and is used for making coats and sports jackets with a country look.

Lambswool A very soft, fine wool taken from lambs before they are seven months old. Lambs wool is often used in high-quality knitwear.

Lamé A fabric woven from metallic threads, usually with another fibre which might be silk or synthetic. It is used for evening wear.

Lawn A very fine fabric, usually made from cotton but also from linen. It is slightly crisper in feel than batiste, and is used to make blouses, shirts and dresses, as well as children's clothes.

Liberty prints Beautiful, exclusive designs printed on to cotton, silk and wool by Liberty of London.

Linen Produced from the stem of the flax plant, this fabric is used for table and bedlinen and fashionable garments.

Lurex The trade name for a metallic thread which can be woven into fabric or knitted, or used as a sewing or embroidery thread.

Lycra The trade name for an elastic fibre. These fibres are used where stretch is needed in swimwear, tights and figure-hugging fashion garments.

Madras cotton A cheap cotton from Madras, India, which is hand woven into brightly coloured checks. The colours are obtained from vegetable dyes and tend to bleed and fade when washed.

Melton A very firm, closely woven wool fabric with a lightly felted finish. It is used for making coats and suits.

Merino Some of the best-quality wool is obtained from the Merino sheep. The name is now sometimes applied to a good-quality woollen fabric.

Mohair Produced from the long hair of the Angora goat, mohair fabric tends to be hairy, but is very warm. It is often mixed with wool to make cloth suitable for suits.

Moiré A finish given to silk and acetate fabrics to produce a watermarked look.

Net An open-mesh fabric where the yarns are knotted rather than woven or knitted. It can be made from silk, cotton or synthetics, and various densities and degrees of softness are available.

Nun's veiling Originally used for religious purposes, this has now become a fashion fabric. It is made from fine wool with an even weave, to create a delicate fabric which can be used to make dresses and blouses.

Nylon A synthetic fibre produced from mineral sources, it is extremely hardwearing and very strong .

Organdie A very fine cotton fabric with a crisp finish, often confused with organza which is the silk equivalent. It is used for interfacing and for party dresses and hats.

Organza Very often confused with its cotton version, organdie, this is a very fine but stiff, crisp fabric with a lot of body. Originally it was made from silk, but there synthetic versions are now available. It is used as an interlining and interfacing, as well as for making ballgowns.

Orlon A trade name for acrylic fibres.

Ottoman A distinctive fabric with wide ridges running across its width, making it quite stiff. Originally made from silk, it is now more likely to be synthetic and is used to make evening wear.

Panné velvet A velvet fabric in which the pile has been pressed flat in one direction, giving it a very shiny, slippery appearance and feel. It is usually synthetic and is used to make evening wear.

Percale A fine, closely woven cotton fabric which has been given a smooth finish. It is widely used to make bedlinen and shirts.

Pima cotton A very fine, good-quality cotton fabric used mainly for making shirts.

Polyester A popular synthetic fibre, it is versatile and can be used in many different ways. It is often mixed with other fibres such as wool and cotton.

Poplin A much-used fabric made from mercerized cotton yarn. It has a slight sheen. It is heavier than lawn and hardwearing; polyester is sometimes added to make it more crease resistant. Poplin is available in plain and printed versions and is used to make dresses, blouses, children's clothes and much more.

Ramie A strong, hardwearing fabric made from a vegetable fibre extracted from ramie grass, which grows in Asia. Ramie is sometimes used to make hats and in dress fabrics when mixed with other fibres.

Satin The name of a weave which gives a smooth, shiny effect on one side of the fabric. It can be made from almost any fibre. Satin has many uses depending on the basic fibre.

Seersucker A fabric with alternate bubbly and tight stripes, which are formed when the fabric is woven and will not iron out. It can be made from cotton or nylon and is used for dresses and children's clothes, and moves in and out of fashion.

Serge A hardwearing, medium-weight twill-weave fabric available in plain colours only. Probably best known for its use in making school uniforms, it is also used for suits.

Shantung A medium-weight silk fabric with a slubby texture that is popular with the fashion conscious for dresses and suits.

Silk Produced by the silk worm, this beautiful fabric comes in a great variety of forms. Used for curtains and soft furnishings, wedding, ballgowns and day wear.

Spandex A polyurethane fabric with a lot of stretch, and therefore used extensively for making swimwear and underwear – in fact, anywhere where stretch is required.

Taffeta Originally made from silk, and now often from synthetics, this is a crisp fabric with a characteristic rustle. Usually produced in brilliant plain colours, taffeta is used to make evening wear and wedding dresses.

Terylene A trade name for polyester fibre.

Tulle A very fine net with tiny holes, which is used mainly for making wedding veils.

Velour A closely woven, heavyweight woollen fabric with a smooth finish, which is used for making coats. The name is now often used for velour jerseys, which are stretchy knitted fabrics with a velvety pile, often made from synthetics and used for casual clothes.

Velvet A fabric with a cut pile which can be made from cotton, synthetics or silk, each having its own characteristics. It is used to make garments for special-occasion wear.

Vicuna Produced from the vicuan llama of South America, it is an expensive and luxurious fabric.

Viscose A type of rayon made from cellulose, the quality of viscose has improved over the years. Can be used on its own to make skirts and dresses or mixed with other fibres for greater versatility.

Voile A fine, lightweight fabric, now made mainly from cotton or synthetics. It is used to produce lightweight, floaty clothing.

Wool Produced from the fleece of the sheep, wool is a very warm and practical fabric used for winter garments.

index

acknowledgments

The author would like to thank Hilary More for her hard work and patience and for writing the instructions for the curtain, cushions, shaped seams and pillow cases and for organising their making up; the team at Quadrille; Liberty of London for their generosity in supplying most of the fabrics; Mary Telford for making up many of the projects so beautifully; Alice Butcher and Lyn Holt at Liberty for their support and kindness; Diana Vernon for all her advice and encouragement; and her long-suffering family: Anthony, Emily, Alice, Nancy and Rupert for being so supportive and understanding.

The publishers would also like to thank Liberty plc and the other companies listed below for their generous help in supplying fabrics:
Liberty plc (pages 29,31,47,53,62,64,89); Bennison (page 42); Calver & Wilson (page 83); Nina Campbell (page 11); Designers Guild (pages 45,57); .
(Panda ribbon, page 29); Malabar (page 69); Ian Mankin (pages 13,73,93, 96); Mulberry Home (page 39); Osborne & Little (pages 11,86; also Beryl Miller for additional making up of projects.

The publisher and photographer also thank Richard Lowther and Lynne Robinson, Lucinda Ganderton and Emma Williams, Amanda Hawkins Knitwear Design, Damask, Diana Digby Ratafiat Hats, Gainsborough Silk Weaving Co. Ltd, Hobbs, Millside Forge, Nina Spooner.